Books written by J

Trust God for Your
What Will Heaven
Never, Never Give Up
How to Study the Bible
Quiet Confidence in the Lord
One Hundred Years from Today
Nuggets of Faith
God's Will for Your Life
Conquering Fear

Books co-authored by Jack and Judy Hartman

God's Joy Regardless of Circumstances
Victory over Adversity
What Does God Say?
Receive Healing from the Lord
Unshakable Faith in Almighty God
Exchange Your Worries for God's Perfect Peace
God's Wisdom Is Available to You
Increased Energy and Vitality

Scripture Meditation Cards co-authored by Jack and Judy Hartman

Receive Healing from the Lord
Freedom from Worry and Fear
Enjoy God's Wonderful Peace
God Is Always with You
Continually Increasing Faith in God
Receive God's Blessings in Adversity
Financial Instructions from God
Find God's Will for Your Life
A Closer Relationship with the Lord
Our Father's Wonderful Love

Comments from Readers
of Our Publications

The following are just a few of the comments contained in almost nine hundred letters we have received pertaining to our publications. For additional comments, see our website: lamplight.net.

Exchange Your Worries for God's Perfect Peace

- "*Exchange Your Worries for God's Perfect Peace* is a masterpiece. I am reading this book to the people here in the Philippines. I saw tears flowing down their faces as I read them parts of this book. I must get this book translated into their language. I am reading this book for the second time. After thirty years in the ministry I have finally learned how to turn my worries over to God. I have learned more from this book in the last few months than I have ever learned in my life. I will not allow my copy of this book to leave my presence. I thank God for you." (Philippines)

- "I just want to tell you how much I appreciate you and your excellent book, *Exchange Your Worries for God's Perfect Peace*. I have read all of your books several times each. I continually go back to refer to the notes I have made in your books. I have done this for close to fifteen years and pages are falling out of your books. I read the Bible daily. Your books are a close second to the Bible. I have never found another Christian author who teaches me more about God's Word and speaks directly to my heart as your writings do. Thank you for helping me appreciate and respect the Word of God." (Wisconsin)

- "I was in despair struggling with my life in ministry. *Exchange Your Worries for God's Perfect Peace* has strengthened me and encouraged my heart. My country is often threatened by disasters. Your book and the Scripture in it has helped me to focus on God, no matter what circumstances I have experienced and will face in the future. The language in the book is very clear and easy to understand for someone like me who uses English as a second language. I have been blessed by reading this book. My faith in Jesus has increased. Thank you for sending this book to me. I thank God that I know you. You are a blessing." (Indonesia)

Victory over Adversity

- "Your book, *Victory over Adversity*, is great. This book is very complete and easy to understand. I liked it so much that I already have read it two times and I will continue to refer to it often. This book has it all. You have done the work for us. Any person facing adversity of any sort can find specific answers from the Bible in your book. I now know that nothing can come against me that God has not already provided for. Thank you so much for your encouragement." (Iowa)

- "I am 84 years old. I am believing God for healing of macular degeneration. I can only read with one eye, but I was so excited about *Victory over Adversity* that I read the entire book with one eye. This book is awesome. I hated to see it come to an end. All of your books have been a great help to me. God bless you." (New Hampshire)

- "Recently a severe problem caused my heart to sink. Fear came into my life. I often woke up in the middle of the night over- whelmed with fear. *Victory over Adversity* was life-saving. This book is another master work. I read Chapter 4 again and again. Chapter 5 helped me to turn this problem over to God Who knows exactly what to do with problems that seem to be impossible to solve. Thank you for lifting my spirits and helping me to see God instead of adversity." (Philippines)

Receive Healing from the Lord

- "Your great book, *Receive Healing from the Lord*, has amazed me. This book has been my daily bread. I have followed all of God's instructions in your book. My children and my wife were healed from severe illness. I was sick myself just before an impor- tant crusade. I meditated on the Scripture in your book for the entire night. I was totally healed. The following day God did won- ders as He healed many people. Since then, people have been coming to receive their healing at our home and church almost every day. Many healings are taking place at our services. This book is wonderful. I am abundantly blessed by it." (Zambia)

- "All of the books that you sent us have been given away. Notable was the testimony of a pastor who was healed as a result of reading *Receive Healing from the Lord.* This brother was in failing health for the last three years. When I met him this year he was really weak. I perceived that numerous worries were choking his faith so I gave him four of your books. The situation of this pastor was quite bad last month. He had mistakenly consumed wrong medication which led to partial blindness and joint pain. He could not move. He called to tell me about his sudden healing. I could not believe it. I was quite apprehensive. I asked him to meet me at the bus station. To my amazement he came riding a bicycle. He narrated to me the story of how he was healed after reading *Receive Healing from the Lord.* This man of God is now strong. It is the Lord. God richly bless you." (Zambia)

- "I am so blessed by your comprehensive book on divine healing. This book is a monumental masterpiece. The Holy Ghost has written this book. Glory be to God that you have obeyed Him. You have presented dynamic scriptural instructions for Christians who are sick that will enable them to progressively increase their faith for divine healing. You obviously have put a lot of labor into this book. Many people will be blessed by it." (Florida)

Trust God for Your Finances
- "We find your material to be so readable and upbuilding. Your writing communicates a clear and fatherly concern for the edification of the believer. *Trust God for Your Finances* is a tremendous book. Your book by far is the most thorough and systematic work I have read to date. The church here in Greece has a great need for this book." (Greece) (This book was translated into Greek.)

- "I have translated *Trust God for Your Finances* into Thai. My pastor asked for 700 copies to distribute at the special yearly conference for pastors. More than 1,000 people attended the conference. Seven hundred copies were distributed to only the pastors, elders and deacons who really wanted the book. After the conference, we had so many calls that another 2,000 copies were printed. Thank you, Mr. Hartman, for this book which is helping so many Thai Christians." (Thailand)

- "Today we had a ministry partner join us for lunch. He said that the book, *Trust God for Your Finances,* that we had translated into Hebrew was the most powerful book he had ever read on the subject. I shared with him the wonderful story of how you shared the book with us and how many Israelis have been enlightened in that area as a result of reading the book. You both are a blessing and a treasure in God's kingdom." (Israel)

What Does God Say?

- "Our Sunday School class meets for two hours each Sunday before the regular church service. We have discussed six or seven of your previous books in past classes. *What Does God Say?* is the best one yet. The response from the people in our class has been phenomenal. We begin each class by asking people to state their biggest problems. Once the problems of the members of the class are defined, we choose which of the 94 topics to discuss. The people in our class are telling other people about this book and new people are joining our class." (Iowa)

- "I have never seen a book like *What Does God Say?*. This is more than a book – it is a complete manual. I am very blessed by the way you have simplified this book. I preach from this book on Sundays, Tuesdays, Fridays and Saturdays. It is always with me so I can preach or teach to any group without notice. I thank God for you and I thank Him for your ministry which has helped many people here." (Zambia)

- "Last year Thailand went through severe political turmoil. As a citizen, my life was turned upside down by the chain of events that disrupted our daily lives. For many months I was distracted, confused and indignant. I did not even know how to pray to God for my country. Then as I read through your book, *What Does God Say?*, I gradually came back to my senses. I studied several topics in this book. I learned to once again put my faith and my concentration on God and His Word. I can feel God's love and peace inside my heart. Thank you, Mr. Hartman, for the light you showed me through your book. You are indeed God's messenger." (Thailand)

Unshakable Faith in Almighty God

- "*Unshakable Faith in Almighty God* has amazed me. The language is so simple and very clear to understand. This book is powerful and life-changing. I will always hang on to this book.

Brother Hartman, God's favour and wisdom are so great on your life. I believe this book is written on very heavy anointing from God. Your reward in heaven will be so great. All those who have sown seeds in your ministry should rejoice. When I wake up, I read this book. Before going to bed, I read it. I will continue to go through it again and again. Your ministry is a big blessing to me. You are always in our prayers." (Zambia)

- "As a minister, missionary and Bible school executive for some sixty years, I would like to comment on your wonderful book, *Unshakable Faith in Almighty God*. You are right on. You are raising a voice that needs to be heard by every Christian in the day in which we live. It is a voice of warning and is also a voice that carries with it a solution for the drama facing the church today. The average Christian is not prepared in the one thing needed to survive the future, an unfailing faith based on saturation in the Word of God." (Florida)

- "If there is one thing that people need above all else it is *Unshakable Faith in Almighty God*. Next to my Bible, I put this book among the best. Every reader should place this book next to his or her Bible. Hundreds of Scripture references that support the challenging truths in this book will equip readers for the future. We want to help get your writings into the hands of people in the island nations. Thank you for being so obedient to the Lord. Thank you for the time and the energy that you have invested in the lives of so many." (Australia)

What Will Heaven Be Like?
- "On the very first page of your book on heaven I was spellbound. The material read so quickly and coherently that it was like having a conversation with a Christian friend. I could really feel the excitement as we talked about the throne of God and its radiance. Those who are curious about heaven will be so delighted and joyful when they read this book. I think the questions at the end of the book are a great idea. This book is a ready-made classroom treasure. I was deeply moved by the gentle loving approach and the manner this material was presented to me, the reader. I can hardly wait to read your other books. You have gained a new fan

and admirer of your special way of presenting the kingdom of heaven and God's love for us." (Mississippi)

- "I came to China from Cambodia where I was a captain in the army. I was a Buddhist. Four weeks before I came to China, I had a dream where Jesus appeared to me. When I woke up the following morning, I looked for Christians to explain more about Jesus Christ to me. After I came to China, I met a Christian man who gave me the book *What Will Heaven Be Like?*. This book answered many questions for me. My English is not very good, but this book is written in very simple English. I have found new life through this book. Please pray for me so that I can share Jesus with my parents and my Buddhist friends when I go back to Cambodia." (China)

- "I am the Youth Director of our church and I'm leading a group of high school students in a Bible study of your book on heaven. We all respect your opinions and have found your book to be an excellent springboard for discussion. It is thought-provoking and informative. This book has much substance and is well organized." (California)

Never, Never Give Up
- "When I received your book *Never, Never Give Up*, all was well in my life. I was supposed to be married when I graduated from the higher institution of learning, but this marriage never materialized. The lady I loved so much suffered from migraine headaches and eye pain. She suffered in great pain for almost a year and then she died. In all of this journey of suffering I read your book three times. The contents are so meaningful to me and built a good strong character in me. Though my fiancé died and went to be with the Lord, God saw me through that problem. *Never, Never Give Up* was a timely book. It is written simply and is easy to understand. I pray that the Lord will continue to use your ministry to help people who are going through a tough time." (Zambia)

- "Thanks for being there when you are so much needed by all of us. After seven major operations I am beginning to walk again and help others which is the full purpose of my existence which Jesus Christ has set before me. Your book, *Never, Never Give Up*, stayed by my pillow along with my Bible while I was recuperating from these operations. When I re-read it, I was charged with peace and energy again. The pain diminishes and I can speak of God's infinite love and mercy to others who are facing similar trials. Thank you for writing this God-inspired book." (Florida)

- "Suicide has shown its face in my mind. I found myself falling deeper and deeper into the pit of hell. My life seemed so grim. I could not see where I could make a difference and was planning to believe that if I chose to leave this life it would not matter. When I received *Never, Never Give Up* I read the first three chapters that evening. When I arrived at page ninety, your verse changed my life. I want you to know that I have been delivered from this season of trial. I rededicated my life to the Lord and feel wonderful. Thank you so much for your work. Through our Lord you have saved my life. Thank you for my life back." (Texas)

Quiet Confidence in the Lord
- "As soon as I was diagnosed with prostate cancer I began to meditate on the Scripture and your explanation of the Scripture in *Quiet Confidence in the Lord.* I carried this book with me everywhere for several weeks. The specialist at the Lahey Clinic in Boston told me I was the calmest person with this diagnosis that he had ever seen. During the pre-op and the surgery a number of people commented on how calm I was. I experienced a lot of discomfort during the difficult first week at home after the surgery. I focused constantly on the Scripture in this wonderful book. I was remarkably calm. Thank you for writing this book that has helped me so much." (Massachusetts)

- "After I graduated from Bible school, I went outside of my country for mission work with my wife. After we were there for nine months, my wife died suddenly. My sorrow was great. I read your book titled *Quiet Confidence in the Lord.* This book spoke to my heart. All twenty-three chapters were written for me. God changed me through this book and comforted me and took away my sorrow. Through the blood of Jesus I entered into God's rest. I can give a great recommendation for this book to anyone who is filled with sorrow and grief. I pray that many people will read this book and develop quiet confidence in the Lord as I did. Thank you so much for sending this book to me. May God bless you and your ministry." (Ethiopia)

- *"Quiet Confidence in the Lord* is with me at work each day. I read and underlined passages that lift my heart and help me to understand something I've known all along and that is that I am not alone and that God cares very much that I'm in the midst of great adversity. I asked God to send me a comforter, someone who would put their arms around me and say, 'I understand and I care.' The answer to that prayer is in you and Judy. Thanks to *Quiet Confidence of the Lord* I am, for the first time in my life, learning to focus on God and not my problems. Thank you both for your ministry. Your books are a tremendous blessing to hurting people all over the world." (Washington, DC)

God's Wisdom Is Available to You

- "I did not sleep last night after reading your book *God's Wisdom is Available to You*. Thank you for your wonderful work. Because of persecution against my ministry, I spent a considerable amount of time in the hospital because of depression. I am now well and healthy in Jesus' name. Thank you for your help. I will be teaching members of my church from key text in your book. Please be my mentor, teacher and counselor." (Ghana)

- "I thank God each and every day for Jack and Judy Hartman. When I started reading your book on wisdom, everything was going wrong in my life. This book revived my spirit and my faith in God. It has changed my life. The Bible used to be like Greek to me. Now I can read it and understand it. I can't put this book down because I know I need to absorb it. I'm going through it for a second time. This book is one of the best things that has ever happened to me. I thank you both and I thank God." (Florida)

- "You did a fantastic job on this book. It is an encyclopedia on God's wisdom. The writing style is just great. Many books don't bring the reader through the subject the way this book does. I'm very impressed with that. You have made it a real joy for me to study and re-digest Scripture. This book has been very good for me." (North Carolina)

How to Study the Bible

- "Your book, *How to Study the Bible*, is a gem. Since I became a Christian 41 years ago, I have studied the Bible using a variety of methods. Your method is simple and straightforward. It involves hard work, but the rewards are real. I have read several of your books and this book is the one I would highly recommend to any Christian because this book is the foundation. God bless you, brother." (England)

- "My wife and I are utilizing the Bible study method that you explained in *How to Study the Bible*. We are really growing spiritually as a result. Our old methods of study were not nearly as fruitful. Thank you for writing about your method." (Idaho)

- "I have read almost all of your books and they are outstanding. The one that blessed me the most was *How to Study the Bible*. The study part was excellent, but the meditation chapters were very, very beneficial. I am indebted to you for sharing these. I purchased 30 copies to give to friends. Every earnest student of God's Word needs a copy." (Tennessee)

Comments on Our Scripture Meditation Cards

- "My back was hurting so badly that I couldn't get comfortable. I was miserable whether I sat or stood or laid down. I didn't know what to do. Suddenly I thought of the Scripture cards on healing that my husband had purchased. I decided to meditate on the Scripture in these cards. I was only on the second card when, all of a sudden, I felt heat go from my neck down through my body. The Lord had healed me. I never knew it could happen so fast. The pain has not come back." (Idaho)

- "My wife and I use your Scripture cards every day when we pray. I read the card for that day in English and then my wife repeats it in Norwegian. We then pray based upon the Scripture reference on that day's card. These cards have been very beneficial to us. We would like to see the Scripture cards published in the Norwegian language." (Norway)

- "Your Scripture cards have been very helpful to my wife and myself. We have taped them to the walls in our home and we meditate on them constantly. I also take four or five cards with me every day when I go to work. I meditate on them while I drive. The Scripture on these cards is a constant source of encouragement to us. We ask for permission to translate *Trust God for Your Finances*. This book is badly needed by the people in Turkey." (This permission was granted.) (Turkey)

- "My mom is 95 years old. She was in the Bergen-Belsen Concentration Camp in Germany from 1943 to 1945. She has always had a lot of worry and fear. My mother was helped greatly in overcoming this problem by your Scripture cards titled *Freedom from Worry and Fear*. She was helped so much that she asked me to order another set to give to a friend." (California)

- "I am overwhelmed about the relevations in your Scripture Meditation Cards. These Scripture cards have helped me so much that I cannot write enough on this sheet of paper. We have gone through a five-day programme in our church using the Scripture cards.

My faith has increased tremendously. I no longer am submitting to my own will and desires, but I am now submitting to the will of God and it is so fantastic. God bless you, Jack and Judy Hartman." (Ghana)

- "I am very enthusiastic about your Scripture cards and your tape titled *Receive Healing from the Lord*. I love your tape. The clarity of your voice and your sincerity and compassion will encourage sick people. They can listen to this tape throughout the day, before they go to sleep at night, while they are driving to the doctor's office, in the hospital, etc. The tape is filled with Scripture and many good comments on Scripture. This cassette tape and your Scripture cards on healing are powerful tools that will help many sick people." (Tennessee) (NOTE: The ten cassette tapes for our Scripture Meditation Cards are available on 80-minute CDs as well.)

- "I meditate constantly on the healing cards and listen to your tape on healing over and over. Your voice is so soothing. You are a wonderful teacher. My faith is increasing constantly." (New Hampshire).

God's Joy Regardless of Circumstances

Jack and Judy Hartman

Lamplight Ministries, Inc.

Dunedin, Florida

Jack and Judy Hartman
Lamplight Ministries, Inc.

PO Box 1307

Dunedin, Florida 34697-2921

Telephone: 1-800-540-1597

FAX: 1-727-784-2980

Website: lamplight.net

Email: lamplight@lamplight.net

ISBN: 978-0-915445-12-7

Library of Congress Control Number: 2009909854

Dedication

Merlin Carothers is the author of many best sellers on the subject of praising God. More than 19 million copies of his books have been printed. These books have been translated into 58 languages. Merlin and his wife, Mary, operate their ministry, the Foundation of Praise, which was established in 1970 in California. Their website is foundationofpraise.org.

Merlin and Mary bring joy to every situation. Judy had the high privilege of being a children's church leader at their church in San Marcos, California in the 1970s. Merlin and Mary live and breathe joy, regardless of the circumstances. They are two of the most joy-filled and peace-filled people on earth. Their lives are dedicated to the spread of the gospel of Jesus Christ.

Merlin and Mary do everything possible to get free books into every state and federal prison in America and into as many city and county jails as possible. They also distribute their publications to military personnel, hospital patients, crisis centers and missionary projects around the world.

Thank you, Merlin and Mary, for bringing praise, thanksgiving and worship of God through His Son, Jesus Christ, into the lives of millions of people all over the world. We love you.

We each began studying the Bible in the *King James Version*. If we could write this entire book with the *King James Version*, we would. However, we want to present the reader with the best possible explanation of each verse of Scripture.

We have carefully reviewed each verse of Scripture in this book to prayerfully select the version of the Bible that we believe will help you to best understand what God is saying to you. In some cases we have used *The New International Version* (NIV) when we believe the language in this particular passage of Scripture will give you more comprehension. In other cases we have used *The Amplified Bible* (AMP) when we believe the amplification will explain more to you.

The *King James Version* (KJV) of the Bible received its name from King James who was the king of England from 1603 to 1625. King James is considered to have been one of the most intellectual and learned kings in the history of Great Britain. He is primarily remembered for authorizing the production of the *King James Version* of the Bible. This English translation from Greek and Hebrew is the most printed book in the history of the world with more than one billion copies in print.

The New International Version (NIV) is the result of the study of a group of approximately one hundred Hebrew and Greek scholars representing more than twenty denominations. This team of scholars devoted ten years to complete the NIV translation. The goal of this committee was to faithfully translate the original Greek, Hebrew and Aramaic biblical text into clearly understandable English. The NIV is the most widely purchased contemporary Bible today.

The Amplified Bible is the result of the study of a group of Bible scholars who spent a total of more than twenty thousand hours amplifying the Bible. They believe that traditional word-by-word translation often fails to reveal the shades of meaning that are part of the original Greek, Hebrew and Aramaic biblical texts.

Any amplification of the original text utilizes brackets for words that clarify the meaning and parentheses for words that contain additional phrases included in the original language. Through this amplification the reader will gain a better understanding of what Hebrew and Greek listeners instinctively understood.

TABLE OF CONTENTS

Introduction

The Bible is filled with many facts about the joy of the Lord. The words "joy," "enjoy," "joyful," "joyous," "rejoice," "rejoices" and "rejoicing" are used more than 450 times in the Bible. There is no question that God created you to live a happy life that is filled with joy. Parents want their children to be happy. Your Father's plan is for you to be happy and filled with joy, regardless of the circumstances you face.

Most people would like to be filled with joy, but very few people know exactly how to receive this tremendous blessing from God. This book contains 551 verses of Scripture that tell you *exactly* and specifically how joy should, can and will come into your heart.

As we begin this book we want to make it very clear that we will give you many instructions that may not make sense to you. Some of the things that we will say in this book may seem almost ridiculous to you. *Will you* make up your mind at the beginning of this book that you will do exactly what the Bible instructs you to do, whether or not these instructions make sense to the limitations of your human understanding?

We recommend that you read this book with a highlighter or a pen. Highlight or underline scriptural facts that are meaningful to you. Write notes in the margins and at the top and bottom of pages pertaining to information that you desire to retain.

You will see the phrase "please highlight or underline" used *many* times throughout this book. We use this phrase to recommend key words from whatever passage of Scripture we are studying.

When you decide to highlight or underline words and to write notes in the margins, you are *studying* the Bible. You then will be prepared for Scripture meditation.

God has instructed you to renew your mind by *studying* the Bible daily (see II Corinthians 4:6 and Ephesians 4:22-24). God also has instructed you to *meditate* day and night on His Word (see Joshua 1:8 and Psalm 1:2-3).

By highlighting or underlining and making notes as you study this Scripture, you will tailor-make this book for yourself. You will know exactly where to go to meditate so that you will experience the joy of the Lord in your life. You will have everything you need from God's supernatural living Word right in front of you, so that you will *not* lose the precious joy that Jesus has given you.

We also want to emphasize that we know there is some repetition in this book and that portions overlap with what we have written in other books. Our model is the Bible. God's Word is filled with repetition because God emphasizes through repetition. There is a great deal of overlapping in the Bible. Many times a passage of Scripture in one Book of the Bible is virtually identical to Scripture from another Book of the Bible.

We do not attempt to be commercially correct in our writing. Our goal is to give you hundreds of specific facts from God's holy Bible that will help *you* when and if you face severe adversity. Difficult times are coming upon the world. We believe that the solid scriptural content of our books will help many people.

God's ways are very different from and very much higher than the ways of the world (see Isaiah 55:8-9). The scriptural instructions in this book will show you exactly what to do to live in supernatural joy, regardless of the circumstances you face.

We are more excited about this book on joy than we have been about any other book we have written. We pray that you will read this book with a completely open mind and that you will be determined to obey the specific instructions your Father has given you so that you will receive His supernatural joy in your life.

WE RECOMMEND THAT YOU
READ THE FIRST FOUR
CHAPTERS OF THIS BOOK AT
ONE TIME, IF POSSIBLE.
WE BELIEVE THAT THESE
CHAPTERS WILL CHANGE THE
LIVES OF MANY PEOPLE.

Chapter 1

Jesus Christ Came from Heaven to Earth for *You*

When you read the first four chapters of this book, you may wonder what all of these scriptural facts have to do with the topic of joy. As these chapters proceed, you will clearly see that the foundation for deep joy in the Lord is a profound sense of *gratitude* to Jesus Christ for the enormous price that He paid for *you*. This price will enable you to live in the joy of the Lord throughout the remainder of your life on earth and, after that, to live in joy throughout eternity in heaven.

People who do not receive Jesus Christ as their Savior will live eternally in hell. The Bible says that the inhabitants of hell will suffer eternally in a furnace of fire (see Psalm 11:6, Matthew 25:41 and Luke 16:23-24). They will have no rest day or night and they will suffer constantly (see Revelation 14:11). The inhabitants of hell will weep and wail and gnash their teeth throughout eternity (see Matthew 13:42).

What exactly determines whether you will suffer throughout eternity in hell or you will live in eternal joy in the glory of heaven? "If anyone's name was not found written in the book of life, he was thrown into the lake of fire." (Revelation 20:15 NIV)

Please highlight or underline the words "anyone" in this verse of Scripture. This word includes *you*. The words "the book of life" in this verse of Scripture refer to the Lamb's Book of Life. The name of every person who has received Jesus Christ as his or her Savior is entered into the Lamb's Book of Life (see Revelation 21:27). Anyone whose name is *not* in this book will suffer eternally in "the lake of fire" which also is called hell.

No matter how good a person may seem, the truth is that *no* person who has ever lived on earth (except for Jesus Christ) has lived a good enough life to live eternally in the glory of heaven. "...None is righteous, just and truthful and upright and conscientious, no, not one." (Romans 3:10 AMP)

Please highlight or underline the words "none" and "no, not one" in this verse of Scripture. *Every* person, with the exception of Jesus Christ, who has ever lived on earth is born with a sin nature and deserves to live eternally in hell. There are *no* exceptions to this statement. "...all have sinned and are falling short of the honor and glory which God bestows and receives." (Romans 3:23 AMP)

Please highlight or underline the words "*all* have sinned" in this verse of Scripture. These words include *you*. You were born separated from God because of Adam and Eve's decision to defy God. If you only commit a few seemingly minor sins in your life, you are just as much of a sinner before God as someone who has sinned grievously on many occasions. "...whosoever keeps the Law [as a] whole but stumbles and offends in one [single instance] has become guilty of [breaking] all of it." (James 2:10 AMP)

In the Old Testament God required a blood sacrifice every year for sins. Animals often were slaughtered to pay the price for the sins of human beings. The New Testament explains that the *only* way the price for the sins of human beings could be paid is for Jesus Christ, Who is God Himself, to become flesh and blood like these human beings. *Only then* could He pay the full price for your sins and for the sins of all human beings. "...it is evident that it was essential that He be made like His brethren in every respect, in order that He might become a merciful (sympathetic) and faithful High Priest in the things related to God, to make atonement and propitiation for the people's sins." (Hebrews 2:17 AMP)

This verse of Scripture speaks of Jesus being "made like His brethren in every respect." This means that He had to pay the price for the sins of all human beings by becoming a flesh and blood human being.

The Bible teaches that an angel came to a young virgin woman named Mary and said, "…Do not be afraid, Mary, for you have found grace (free, spontaneous, absolute favor and loving-kindness) with God. And listen! You will become pregnant and will give birth to a Son, and you shall call His name Jesus. He will be great (eminent) and will be called the Son of the Most High; and the Lord God will give to Him the throne of His forefather David, and He will reign over the house of Jacob throughout the ages; and of His reign there will be no end. And Mary said to the angel, How can this be, since I have no [intimacy with any man as a] husband? Then the angel said to her, The Holy Spirit will come upon you, and the power of the Most High will overshadow you [like a shining cloud]; and so the holy (pure, sinless) Thing (Offspring) which shall be born of you will be called the Son of God." (Luke 1:30-35 AMP)

The name of Jesus is a holy name. Jesus was not the name that Mary decided to name her son. The name of Jesus came directly from heaven. Mary was directed by this angel to name her son Jesus.

You also must understand the importance of Jesus Christ being born of a virgin. If Jesus was born from a human father and mother, He would be a descendant of Adam. He would inherit the sin of Adam as every person who has lived since Adam has done.

Jesus could only redeem *you* from your sins if He was a flesh and blood human being who was not a descendant of Adam. The only way that this unique goal could be accomplished was to have Mary's pregnancy caused by the Holy Spirit.

Because Mary was a virgin, Jesus is the *only* person Who has ever lived who was not a descendant of Adam. Therefore, Jesus was able to be the Messiah that the Jewish people had been expecting.

Jesus was a Jew sent by God to save His people from their sins. "…you shall call His name Jesus [the Greek form of the Hebrew Joshua, which means Savior], for He will save His people from their sins …" (Matthew 1:21 AMP)

Jesus Christ left the glory of heaven to come to earth to be *your* Savior. God loves *you* so much that He sent His only Son to pay the *full price* for *every* sin you have ever committed so that *you* can live eternally with Him in heaven. "For God so loved the world, that he gave his only begotten Son, that whosoever believeth in him should not perish, but have everlasting life." (John 3:16 KJV)

You must know and believe that Jesus Christ has paid the full price for your sins. There is *no other* way to eternal salvation. Jesus said, "…I am the way and the truth and the life. No one comes to the Father except through me." (John 14:6 NIV)

Please highlight or underline the words "no one" in this verse of Scripture. The *only* way that you can live eternally in the joy of heaven is to receive Jesus Christ as your Savior.

Adam and Eve were created by Jesus Christ and given the ability to have children. "In the beginning [before all time] was the Word (Christ), and the Word was with God, and the Word was God Himself. He was present originally with God. All things were made and came into existence through Him; and without Him was not even one thing made that has come into being." (John 1:1-3 AMP)

Please highlight or underline the words "In the beginning [before all time]" in this passage of Scripture. Jesus Christ has always existed. *Jesus Christ is "God Himself."* Jesus created all living things; they were created with the ability to reproduce themselves.

This statement is almost inconceivable. Just think that the same Jesus Christ Who created every person on earth came to this earth as a human being. Jesus Christ, God Himself, humbled Himself to be born in a lowly manger surrounded by animals to pay the full price for *your* sin.

You should be humbled by your awareness of the price that Jesus paid for you. "Let this same attitude and purpose and [humble] mind be in you which was in Christ Jesus: [Let Him be your example in humility:] Who, although being essentially one with God and in the form of God [possessing the fullness of the attributes which make God God], did not think this equality with God was a thing to be eagerly grasped or retained, but stripped Himself [of all privileges and rightful dignity], so as to assume the guise of a servant (slave), in that He became like men and was born a human being. And after He had appeared in human form, He abased and humbled Himself [still further] and carried His obedience to the extreme of death, even the death of the cross!" (Philippians 2:5-8 AMP)

Please highlight or underline the words "being essentially one with God" and "equality with God" in this passage of Scripture. Jesus Christ is one with God. He is *equal to* God. Jesus humbled Himself from being one with God to become a "servant (slave)" so that you can live eternally with Him in heaven.

Jesus willingly left heaven to be born on earth as a baby. In heaven Jesus was known and recognized as God. On earth He was considered a mere man until He began to exercise His tremendous anointing.

Jesus took upon Himself the form of a *slave* because He willingly gave up His life to pay the full price for *your* sin. He enslaved Himself so that you can be completely set free from sin.

If you are not absolutely certain that you will live eternally in heaven, please stop reading this chapter now and turn to the Appendix on page 225. Read the Scripture in the Appendix carefully. *Do exactly what the holy Bible instructs you to do so that you will be absolutely certain that you will live eternally in heaven. Welcome to the family of God!*

Salvation and redemption are a *gift* from God that you must choose to receive. God gave you a free will. You must willingly choose to become His child through the gift of His Son, Jesus Christ.

In this chapter we have established a scriptural foundation to show you clearly Who Jesus Christ is and that He willingly humbled Himself to come to earth to pay for your sin. *Is your heart filled with gratitude to Jesus* based on these undeniable truths that you have just read? If your heart is filled with gratitude now, you will be even more grateful when you read additional truths in the next three chapters about the supreme sacrifice that Jesus Christ made for *you*.

Chapter 2

Jesus Went through an Enormous Ordeal

We now are ready to look at what the Bible teaches about how much Jesus Christ was willing to humble Himself to pay the full price for every sin you have ever committed. Throughout the next three chapters you will read many truths about the final days of the earthly ministry of Jesus Christ.

Jesus and His disciples ate a Passover dinner in an upper room in Jerusalem shortly before Jesus was to be crucified. After this dinner Jesus and His disciples climbed the Mount of Olives to a garden on the side of the mountain that is called the Garden of Gethsemane. "They went to a place called Gethsemane, and Jesus said to his disciples, 'Sit here while I pray.' He took Peter, James and John along with him, and he began to be deeply distressed and troubled. 'My soul is overwhelmed with sorrow to the point of death,' he said to them. 'Stay here and keep watch.'" (Mark 14:32-34 NIV)

Know that Jesus Christ Who is equal to God and one with God was "deeply distressed and troubled" regarding the price He was about to pay for *you*. Jesus said, "My soul is overwhelmed with sorrow to the point of death."

Think of the enormity of what Jesus went through in the Garden of Gethsemane. "And going a little farther, He fell on the ground and kept praying that if it were possible the [fatal] hour might pass from Him. And He was saying, Abba, [which means] Father, everything is possible for You. Take away this cup from Me; yet not what I will, but what You [will]." (Mark 14:35-36 AMP)

Jesus Christ is referred to many times in the Bible as the "Son of man." Jesus still was the Son of God, but He came to earth as a human being with the same ability to think and feel that you have.

As Jesus fully understood from His human perspective the magnitude of the price that He was about to pay for *you,* He threw Himself on the ground. He fell on the ground in prayer, asking God if He would take this enormous price away from Him. Is your heart becoming more and more filled with gratitude as you begin to understand the enormous price that Jesus Christ paid for *you*?

In spite of His realization of the price that He would have to pay, Jesus said, "not what I will, but what You [will]." Even though Jesus asked God if this price could be removed, He asserted that He still desired to do what God wanted, even though in His humanity He was suffering with the weight of the heavy burden that He was about to carry for *you.*

Jesus asked Peter, James and John, the three disciples who went with Him to Gethsemane, to stay awake and watch with Him. In spite of this request, the disciples fell asleep. "...He came back and found them sleeping, and He said to Peter, Simon, are you asleep? Have you not the strength to keep awake and watch [with Me for] one hour? Keep awake and watch and pray [constantly], that you may not enter into temptation; the spirit indeed is willing, but the flesh is weak. He went away again and prayed, saying the same words. And again He came back and found them sleeping, for their eyes were very heavy; and they did not know what answer to give Him." (Mark 14:37-40 AMP)

We receive additional insight into what Jesus went through in the Garden of Gethsemane in the Book of Luke. After going off by Himself three different times and throwing Himself on the ground, Jesus agonized so much that His sweat became like blood. "And there appeared to Him an angel from heaven, strengthening Him in spirit. And being in an agony [of mind], He prayed [all the] more earnestly and intently, and His sweat became like great clots of blood dropping down upon the ground." (Luke 22:43-44 AMP)

God sent an angel to help Jesus because He was going through such agony. Jesus agonized so much that "His sweat became like great clots of blood dropping down upon the ground."

Sweating blood is called haematidrosis which is a condition where the stress is so great that a person's blood vessels break and blood is secreted through the sweat glands. Try to understand how much Jesus agonized over the price that He was about to pay for *you.*

After all of this agonizing Jesus was ready to pay the supreme price that will enable you to live in joy throughout the remainder of your life on earth and throughout eternity in heaven. "And He came back a third time and said to them, Are you still sleeping and resting? It is enough [of that]! The hour has come. The Son of Man is betrayed into the hands of sinful men (men whose way or nature is to act in opposition to God). Get up, let us be going! See, My betrayer is at hand!" (Mark 14:41-42 AMP)

Jesus had been betrayed by one of His beloved disciples, Judas Iscariot. After going through this tremendous ordeal in the Garden of Gethsemane, Jesus saw that Judas had arrived with a crowd of armed men. "And at once, while He was still speaking, Judas came, one of the Twelve [apostles], and with him a crowd of men with swords and clubs, [who came] from the chief priests and the scribes and the elders [of the Sanhedrin]." (Mark 14:43 AMP)

Jesus then was brought before a Jewish high priest named Annas who questioned Jesus about the things that He had been teaching. Annas and his followers did not like the answers that Jesus gave. "…one of the officials nearby struck him in the face. 'Is this the way you answer the high priest?' he demanded." (John 18:22 NIV)

Can you imagine Jesus Christ, Creator of the heavens and the earth, being hit in the face because He answered questions truthfully? This is just one more example of the enormous price Jesus paid so that *you* can live eternally with Him in the glory of heaven.

Jesus then was sent before the Sanhedrin which was the Jewish Supreme Court. This meeting was held at approximately 4:00 a.m. The goal of this court was to find people who would *tell lies* in order to justify the execution of Jesus. "Now the chief priests and the whole council (the Sanhedrin) sought to get false witnesses to testify against

Jesus, so that they might put Him to death; but they found none, though many witnesses came forward [to testify]..." (Matthew 26:59-60 AMP)

Please highlight or underline the words "false witnesses to testify against Jesus" in this passage of Scripture. The corrupt Jewish Supreme Court "found none." They could not even find one witness to lie about Jesus.

The Sanhedrin continued to question Jesus. When they asked Him whether He was the Son of God, Jesus said that He was. "Then the high priest tore his clothes and exclaimed, He has uttered blasphemy! What need have we of further evidence? You have now heard His blasphemy. What do you think now? They answered, He deserves to be put to death. Then they spat in His face and struck Him with their fists; and some slapped Him in the face" (Matthew 26:65-67 AMP)

The high priest was so infuriated with the answer that Jesus gave that he actually "tore his clothes." He worked himself into a frenzy. His associates "spat in His face and struck Him with their fists; and some slapped Him in the face." Once again you can clearly see the ordeal that Jesus experienced so that *you* can live eternally with Him in heaven.

This trial before the Sanhedrin was a travesty. There were no witnesses for the defense. There was no cross examination. Jesus was exhausted. He had been awake all night after going through the severe ordeal of sweating blood in the Garden of Gethsemane. The Sanhedrin found Jesus to be guilty of blasphemy because He said that He was the Son of God. Jesus was sentenced to death because He told the truth.

The Sanhedrin then had Jesus put in chains. They took Him to the Roman governor because the Sanhedrin could not carry out a death sentence without the approval of Pontius Pilate, the Roman governor of Judea. Pilate happened to be visiting in Jerusalem, so the Jews took Jesus to him at the royal palace. Pilate questioned Jesus. Pilate then sent Jesus to Herod who was the leader of the Jews.

Jesus must have been exhausted by this time. He had not had any sleep. People had spit on Him, beaten Him and shackled Him with chains as they dragged Him back and forth across Jerusalem throughout the night.

Herod was a foolish and fickle man who asked Jesus many absurd questions. Herod, like Pilate, did *not* find Jesus guilty. He sent Jesus back across town to Pilate. "…Herod, with his soldiers, treated Him with contempt and scoffed at and ridiculed Him; then, dressing Him up in bright and gorgeous apparel, he sent Him back to Pilate." (Luke 23:11 AMP)

The travesty continued. "Pilate then called together the chief priests and the rulers and the people, and said to them, You brought this Man before me as One Who was perverting and misleading and turning away and corrupting the people; and behold, after examining Him before you, I have not found any offense (crime or guilt) in this Man in regard to your accusations against Him; no, nor indeed did Herod, for he sent Him back to us; behold, He has done nothing deserving of death. I will therefore chastise Him and deliver Him amended (reformed, taught His lesson) and release Him." (Luke 23:13-16 AMP)

No one found Jesus guilty of *anything*. Pilate said that he was going to release Jesus. The Jewish people who surrounded Pilate were in a frenzy. They wanted Jesus to be killed. They were not willing to settle for anything less. "…the Jews kept shrieking, If you release this Man, you are no friend of Caesar! Anybody who makes himself [out to be] a king sets himself up against Caesar [is a rebel against the emperor]!" (John 19:12 AMP)

Pilate apparently was afraid that the Jewish leaders would complain to Caesar and that he would lose his job. He did not want to kill a man who was not guilty. Pilate's custom was to release one Jewish prisoner each year at the Passover. He proposed that Jesus be set free on this basis.

The mob in the courtyard was indignant. They said that Pilate should release a prisoner, but that he should release a prisoner named Barabbas. "…the chief priests and the elders prevailed on the people to ask for Barabbas, and put Jesus to death. Again the governor said to them, Which of the two do you wish me to release for you? And they said, Barabbas! Pilate said to them, Then what shall I do with Jesus Who is called Christ? They all replied, Let Him be crucified!

And he said, Why? What has He done that is evil? But they shouted all the louder, Let Him be crucified!" (Matthew 27:20 AMP)

You can see how unjustly Jesus was treated throughout the travesty of His questioning by various government officials. Pilate was completely frustrated. He finally gave in. "…when Pilate saw that he was getting nowhere, but rather that a riot was about to break out, he took water and washed his hands in the presence of the crowd, saying, I am not guilty of nor responsible for this righteous Man's blood; see to it yourselves. And all the people answered, Let His blood be on us and on our children! So he set free for them Barabbas; and he [had] Jesus whipped, and delivered Him up to be crucified." (Matthew 27:24-26 AMP)

Pilate attempted to absolve himself of blame. Now that you have seen what Jesus went through for you during His "trials," we are ready to look in detail at the tremendous price that Jesus Christ paid for *you* as He was whipped, beaten and crucified.

Chapter 3

Jesus Died to Pay the Price for *Your* Sins

Pontius Pilate ordered Jesus to be flogged with a leaded whip. This type of whipping is called scourging which means to whip the bare back of a person with a lash containing several leather thongs that are weighted with lead pellets and sharp pieces of bone. Scourging was such a severe form of punishment that Roman law limited it to a maximum of 39 strokes with a whip. Even so, most people fainted because of the pain. Some people died because of scourging.

Jesus was stripped of His clothes before He was flogged by Roman soldiers. His hands were tied to an upright post. His back, buttocks and legs were flogged by the soldiers. Jesus undoubtedly lost a great deal of blood because of this whipping. He may have become unconscious.

How badly was the Son of God whipped for *you*? "[For many the Servant of God became an object of horror; many were astonished at Him.] His face and His whole appearance were marred more than any man's, and His form beyond that of the sons of men..." (Isaiah 52:14 AMP)

Jesus was whipped *so badly* that He "became an object of horror." He took whip lashes across His face for *you*. Onlookers were "astonished" at how badly Jesus had been whipped.

This terrible whipping was only the beginning of the price that Jesus was about to pay. "Then the soldiers led Him away to the court-yard inside the palace, that is, the Praetorium, and they called the entire detachment of soldiers together. And they dressed Him in [a] purple [robe], and, weaving together a crown of thorns, they placed it on Him. And they began to salute Him, Hail (greetings, good health to You, long life to You), King of the Jews! And they struck His head with a staff made of a [bamboo-like] reed and spat on Him and kept bowing their knees in homage to Him. And when they had [finished] making sport of Him, they took the purple [robe] off of Him and put His own clothes on Him. And they led Him out [of the city] to crucify Him." (Mark 15:16-20 AMP)

Jesus Christ, the Son of God, was ridiculed. He then was beaten on the head with a piece of wood. The Roman soldiers spat on Him. They then led Him on an excruciating journey through the streets of Jerusalem.

Consider how weary Jesus must have been. He had agonized in the Garden of Gethsemane. He had been arrested and went through several unfair trials before Jewish and Roman authorities. He suffered through a horrible whipping. He was mocked, insulted, beaten and spat upon. He went through all of this ordeal with absolutely no sleep. He was exhausted, weary, beaten, bloodied and disfigured.

The Son of God then was forced to walk through the streets of Jerusalem carrying the transverse beam of the cross that would be used to crucify Him. The Romans kept the upright part of the cross as a permanent fixture at the place of crucifixion. Each prisoner had to carry the crosspiece to the place of his crucifixion.

The crosspiece had to be heavy enough to support the weight of a man. It was probably about six feet long and weighed approximately one hundred pounds. The heavy crosspiece probably was placed across the neck and shoulders of Jesus. His arms and His body were tied to this piece of the cross that would be used for His crucifixion.

The Roman soldiers normally took people who were about to crucified through the busiest streets of Jerusalem to serve as an example to the people. After everything He had been through, Jesus must have had a problem just walking, let alone attempting to carry a heavy piece of wood. He probably stumbled and fell.

We do not know for certain, but the Bible says that a man was requested to follow behind Jesus, carrying the crosspiece of His cross for Him. "…as they led him away, they laid hold upon one Simon, a Cyrenian, coming out of the country, and on him they laid the cross, that he might bear it after Jesus." (Luke 23:26 KJV)

This procession of people arrived late in the morning at the place of execution. "And when they were come to the place, which is called Calvary, there they crucified him…" (Luke 23:33 KJV)

The Book of Mark used another name for the place where Jesus was to be crucified. "And they led Him to Golgotha [in Latin: Calvary], meaning The Place of a Skull." (Mark 15:22 AMP)

Golgotha was the Hebrew word for the place where Jesus was crucified. Calvary was the Latin word for the place of His crucifixion. The words Golgotha and Calvary refer to the same place. No one knows exactly where the crucifixion took place, but many Bible scholars believe that Jesus was crucified on a hill outside of Jerusalem that is shaped like a skull.

When they reached the place of crucifixion, Jesus was offered some medicated wine to deaden the excruciating pain that He soon would experience. Jesus refused this wine. He chose to suffer with His mind clear and fully conscious. "There they offered Jesus wine to drink, mixed with gall; but after tasting it, he refused to drink it." (Matthew 27:34 NIV)

Jesus was thrown to the ground, lying on His back with His arms stretched out across the crossbeam that He and Simon had carried across Jerusalem. Large spikes that were approximately seven inches long were driven into His wrists. Then Bible says that nails were driven into His hands, but studies have shown that nails driven into the ligaments and bones of a person's hand could not possibly support the weight of the body during crucifixion. In ancient terminology, the wrist was considered part of the hand.

When Jesus was thrown to the ground, the wounds that He suffered from scourging probably were torn open and contaminated with dirt. Jesus must have been perspiring. These open wounds undoubtedly were extremely uncomfortable.

After His wrists were nailed to the crossbar, Jesus and the crossbar then were lifted onto the permanent upright portion of the cross.

Probably three or four soldiers were required to do this. These soldiers then nailed His ankles to the cross with more large spikes.

Crucifixion was such a severe method of punishment that caused such excruciating pain and suffering that Roman citizens could *not* be crucified. Only slaves and the lowest type of criminals could be crucified. When people were crucified, insects often fed on the open wounds from the flogging that always preceded a crucifixion.

Hundreds of years before Jesus was crucified, the psalmist David prophesied about the scene that would take place at this time. "...[like a pack of] dogs they have encompassed me; a company of evildoers has encircled me, they pierced my hands and my feet. I can count all my bones; [the evildoers] gaze at me." (Psalm 22:16-17 AMP)

Jesus Christ paid this horrible price for *you*. "...Christ suffered for you, leaving you an example, that you should follow in his steps. He committed no sin, and no deceit was found in his mouth. When they hurled their insults at him, he did not retaliate; when he suffered, he made no threats. Instead, he entrusted himself to him who judges justly. He himself bore our sins in his body on the tree, so that we might die to sins and live for righteousness; by his wounds you have been healed." (I Peter 2:21-24 NIV)

Even though Jesus suffered horribly on the cross, He did not complain. He did not respond to the people who insulted Him. Jesus thought of others instead of thinking of Himself.

He thought of His mother who stood next to the cross weeping. He asked His disciple, John, to take care of her. "Near the cross of Jesus stood his mother, his mother's sister, Mary the wife of Clopas, and Mary Magdalene. When Jesus saw his mother there, and the disciple whom he loved standing nearby, he said to his mother, 'Dear woman, here is your son,' and to the disciple, 'Here is your mother.' From that time on, this disciple took her into his home." (John 19:25-27 NIV)

When one of the two thieves who were crucified with Jesus accepted Him as Lord, Jesus told this thief that he would be with Him in Paradise that day. "One of the criminals who was suspended kept up a railing at Him, saying, Are You not the Christ (the Messiah)? Rescue Yourself and us [from death]! But the other one reproved him, saying, Do you not even fear God, seeing you yourself are under the same sentence of condemnation and suffering the same penalty? And we indeed suffer it justly, receiving the due reward of our actions; but this Man has done nothing out of the way [nothing strange or eccentric or perverse or unreasonable]. Then he said to Jesus, Lord, remember me when You come in Your kingly glory! And He answered him, Truly I tell you, today you shall be with Me in Paradise." (Luke 23:39-43 AMP)

As Jesus Christ, the Son of God, hung on the cross, He looked down at the Roman soldiers who had put Him there. They were dividing His clothing into equal portions.

The soldiers gambled to see who would get His seamless robe. "Then the soldiers, when they had crucified Jesus, took His garments and made four parts, one share for each soldier, and also the tunic (the long shirtlike undergarment). But the tunic was seamless, woven [in one piece] from the top throughout. So they said to one another, Let us not tear it, but let us cast lots to decide whose it shall be. This was to fulfill the Scripture, They parted My garments among them, and for My clothing they cast lots. So the soldiers did these things." (John 19:23-24 AMP)

When Jesus was crucified, He did not rant and rave at the soldiers who crucified Him the way that many people who were crucified did. Instead, Jesus looked down at the soldiers who crucified Him and said, "Father, forgive them; for they know not what they do." (Luke 23:34 KJV)

The entire world was covered with darkness during the three hours that Jesus was on the cross. "Now from the sixth hour (noon) there was darkness over all the land until the ninth hour (three o'clock)." (Matthew 27:45 AMP)

You can see the mighty hand of God in both the birth and death of Jesus Christ. The birth of Jesus was proclaimed by a bright star that drew wise men to Jerusalem to worship Him (see Matthew 2:1-2). There was no light in the entire world when Jesus died.

Jesus was separated from His Father as this three hour period drew to a close. "And about the ninth hour (three o'clock) Jesus cried with a loud voice, Eli, Eli, lama sabachthani? – that is, My God, My

God, why have You abandoned Me [leaving Me helpless, forsaking and failing Me in My need]?" (Matthew 27:46 AMP)

Please highlight or underline the words "abandoned" and "leaving Me helpless, forsaking and failing Me in My need" in this verse of Scripture and the amplification. These words were fulfillment of a prophecy that was made many years before by the psalmist David who said, "My God, my God, why have You forsaken me? Why are You so far from helping me, and from the words of my groaning?" (Psalm 22:1 AMP)

Jesus experienced the worst agony of all when the sins of the world separated Him from His Father. In addition to the excruciating pain and overwhelming fatigue, Jesus knew that He had been completely abandoned by His beloved Father.

Why did God turn His back on Jesus at this time? God turned His back on Jesus because, *in addition to* the horrible physical ordeal of crucifixion, Jesus Christ actually *became sin*. When He was crucified, Jesus took upon Himself the sins of the entire world. "God made him who had no sin to be sin for us, so that in him we might become the righteousness of God." (II Corinthians 5:21 NIV)

Please highlight or underline the words "to be sin for us" in this verse of Scripture. Even though Jesus lived a perfect life and never sinned, He actually *became sin*. He took *your* sin upon Himself and the sins of every other person who would ever live from that point forward. Doing this caused separation from God Who cannot look upon sin. Jesus suffered this separation from God so that *you* would never be separated from God.

Jesus died voluntarily. God gave Him the authority to die and also the authority to be raised from the dead. He was *not* killed by the soldiers. Jesus said, "...I lay down My [own] life – to take it back again. No one takes it away from Me. On the contrary, I lay it down voluntarily. [I put it from Myself.] I am authorized and have power to lay it down (to resign it) and I am authorized and have power to take it back again. These are the instructions (orders) which I have received [as My charge] from My Father." (John 10:17-18 AMP)

Jesus did exactly what His Father had instructed Him to do. He then said three glorious and triumphant words in the final moments before He died. He said, "...It is finished..." (John 19:30 KJV)

His mission was accomplished. Jesus Christ died as a *Victor*. "...Jesus, crying out with a loud voice, said, Father, into Your hands I commit My spirit! And with these words, He expired." (Luke 23:46 AMP)

Please note that Jesus cried out "with a loud voice." Even though He had been through such an excruciating ordeal since the Garden of Gethsemane the night before, the loud voice that Jesus spoke with indicates that His inner man was strong right up to the end. He spoke with power and authority.

When Jesus committed His spirit to God, He and His Father were back together. The price for *your* redemption had been paid in full. At this precise moment a miracle took place at the curtain of the temple in Jerusalem. A large and strong curtain covered the entrance to the Holy of Holies which was the innermost portion of the Temple.

When Jesus dismissed His spirit, the curtain was split wide open. "And the curtain [of the Holy of Holies] of the temple was torn in two from top to bottom. And when the centurion who stood facing Him saw Him expire this way, he said, Really, this Man was God's Son!" (Mark 15:38-39 AMP)

When this curtain was split, the Old Testament had ended and a new era had begun. Elaborate ceremonies no longer would be necessary to approach God. From this moment on, *every* person who accepts Jesus Christ as his or her Savior *receives personal access to God.*

In addition to splitting the curtain from top to bottom, God also shook the hills around Jerusalem with an earthquake. Rocks split in two. Graves opened. Believers who had died rose out of their graves. "The tombs were opened and many bodies of the saints who had fallen asleep in death were raised [to life]" (Matthew 27:52 AMP)

People being raised from the dead was a preview of what would be available from this point forward to *you* and to every person who received Jesus Christ as his or her Savior. *Know* that every aspect of the supreme price that Jesus paid that you have read about in this chapter was paid for *you*. Your heart should *overflow with gratitude* because of the tremendous price that Jesus Christ paid for *you*.

Chapter 4

Jesus Won a Total Victory

This is the final chapter that is filled with specific facts that tell you exactly why your heart should overflow with joy because of your deep gratitude for the enormous price that Jesus Christ paid for *you*.

After the death of Jesus one of His followers asked for and received permission to put His body into a tomb. "As evening approached, there came a rich man from Arimathea, named Joseph, who had himself become a disciple of Jesus. Going to Pilate, he asked for Jesus' body, and Pilate ordered that it be given to him. Joseph took the body, wrapped it in a clean linen cloth, and placed it in his own new tomb that he had cut out of the rock. He rolled a big stone in front of the entrance to the tomb and went away. Mary Magdalene and the other Mary were sitting there opposite the tomb." (Matthew 27:57-61 NIV)

Both the Jewish leaders and the Pharisees were concerned that some trick would be played with the body of Jesus. They insisted that the tomb must be sealed. Guards were posted around it. "The next day, the one after Preparation Day, the chief priests and the Pharisees went to Pilate. 'Sir,' they said, 'we remember that while he was still alive that deceiver said, 'After three days I will rise again.' So give the order for the tomb to be made secure until the third day. Otherwise, his disciples may come and steal the body and tell the people that he has been raised from the dead. This last deception will be worse than the first.' 'Take a guard,' Pilate answered. 'Go, make the tomb as secure as you know how.' So they went and made the tomb secure by putting a seal on the stone and posting the guard." (Matthew 27:62-66 NIV)

Jesus was placed in the tomb on Friday afternoon. On the Sunday morning when we today celebrate the Resurrection of Jesus Christ, two women went to the tomb.

These women saw the greatest miracle of all time. "After the Sabbath, at dawn on the first day of the week, Mary Magdalene and the other Mary went to look at the tomb. There was a violent earthquake, for an angel of the Lord came down from heaven and, going to the tomb, rolled back the stone and sat on it. His appearance was like lightning, and his clothes were white as snow. The guards were so afraid of him that they shook and became like dead men. The angel said to the women, "Do not be afraid, for I know that you are looking for Jesus, who was crucified. He is not here; he has risen, just as he said. Come and see the place where he lay. Then go quickly and tell his disciples: 'He has risen from the dead and is going ahead of you into Galilee. There you will see him.' Now I have told you." (Matthew 28:1-7 NIV)

This passage of Scripture contains the essence of the facts pertaining to the victory that Jesus won for *you*. Jesus rose from the dead just as He said He would. When He rose from the dead, this supernatural act sealed the total victory that Jesus won for *you* throughout your life on earth, when you die and throughout eternity in heaven.

This angel brought a magnificent message from God. By raising Jesus from the dead, God proved that Jesus Christ is His Son just as Jesus said He was. "…[as to His divine nature] according to the Spirit of holiness was openly designated the Son of God in power [in a striking, triumphant and miraculous manner] by His resurrection from the dead, even Jesus Christ our Lord (the Messiah, the Anointed One)." (Romans 1:4 AMP)

Please highlight or underline the words "by His resurrection from the dead" in this verse of Scripture. When Jesus rose from the dead, His victory was total, complete and absolute. He had achieved everything His Father had sent Him to earth to accomplish.

Jesus won a glorious victory. He passed this victory on to *you*. "…if, by the trespass of the one man, death reigned through that one man, how much more will those who receive God's abundant provision of grace and of the gift of righteousness reign in life through the one man, Jesus Christ." (Romans 5:17 NIV)

Please highlight or underline the words "by the trespass of the one man, death reigned through that one man" in this verse of Scripture. These words refer to the sin of Adam in the Garden of Eden which gave the death of a human being power that never before existed. Because of the sin of Adam and Eve, men and women no longer lived without sin. Death became part of human existence.

Please highlight or underline the words "reign in life" in this verse of Scripture. Jesus Christ won a total victory over death. He also enabled you to reign in life and to live continually in His joy because of the blood He shed for you. You reign in life over every circumstance because Jesus lives inside of you.

Even though you have just read about the victory that Jesus won, Mary Magdalene and His disciples did not yet understand what had taken place. They were still mourning Jesus. "Early on the first day of the week, while it was still dark, Mary Magdalene went to the tomb and saw that the stone had been removed from the entrance. So she came running to Simon Peter and the other disciple, the one Jesus loved, and said, 'They have taken the Lord out of the tomb, and we don't know where they have put him!'" (John 20:1-2 NIV)

Mary Magdalene and the disciples were startled. They did not know what had happened. "...Peter and the other disciple started for the tomb. Both were running, but the other disciple outran Peter and reached the tomb first. He bent over and looked in at the strips of linen lying there but did not go in. Then Simon Peter, who was behind him, arrived and went into the tomb. He saw the strips of linen lying there, as well as the burial cloth that had been around Jesus' head. The cloth was folded up by itself, separate from the linen. Finally the other disciple, who had reached the tomb first, also went inside. He saw and believed. (They still did not understand from Scripture that Jesus had to rise from the dead.)" (John 20:3-9 NIV)

The disciples had no conception of the enormous victory that had been won by the resurrection of Jesus Christ. Mary Magdalene did not understand either. "...Mary stood outside the tomb crying. As she wept, she bent over to look into the tomb and saw two angels in white, seated where Jesus' body had been, one at the head and the other at the foot. They asked her, 'Woman, why are you crying?'" (John 20:10-13 NIV)

Mary's tears soon would be turned to joy. "'They have taken my Lord away,' she said, 'and I don't know where they have put him.' At this, she turned around and saw Jesus standing there, but she did not realize that it was Jesus. 'Woman,' he said, 'why are you crying? Who is it you are looking for?' Thinking he was the gardener, she said, 'Sir, if you have carried him away, tell me where you have put him, and I will get him.' Jesus said to her, 'Mary.' She turned toward him and cried out in Aramaic, 'Rabboni!' (which means Teacher). Jesus said, 'Do not hold on to me, for I have not yet returned to the Father. Go instead to my brothers and tell them, 'I am returning to my Father and your Father, to my God and your God.'" (John 20:14-17 NIV)

For the first time Mary understood that Jesus *actually had risen from the dead* just as He said He would. "Mary Magdalene went to the disciples with the news: 'I have seen the Lord!' And she told them that he had said these things to her. On the evening of that first day of the week, when the disciples were together, with the doors locked for fear of the Jews, Jesus came and stood among them and said, 'Peace be with you!' After he said this, he showed them his hands and side. The disciples were overjoyed when they saw the Lord." (John 20:18-20 NIV)

Please highlight or underline the words "with the doors locked for fear of the Jews, Jesus came and stood among them" in this passage of Scripture. *How* was Jesus able to come to the disciples and talk with them when all of the doors were locked?

Jesus was able to do this because of the super natural victory He won when He rose from the dead. Nothing on earth, locked doors or anything else, can override the power of this supernatural victory that Jesus Christ won for *you.*

One of the disciples, Thomas, was not there. Have you ever heard the term "Doubting Thomas?" The following passage of Scripture explains the reason for this expression. "Now Thomas (called Didymus), one of the Twelve, was not with the disciples when Jesus came. So the other disciples told him, 'We have seen the Lord!' But he said to them, 'Unless I see the nail marks in his hands and put my finger where the nails were, and put my hand into his side, I will not believe it.'" (John 20:24-25 NIV)

Thomas was like many people are today. They will not believe unless they can see first. Even though the other disciples described the resurrection of Jesus, Thomas was skeptical. For eight days the other disciples talked excitedly about the return of Jesus, but Thomas still had to be shown. "A week later his disciples were in the house again, and Thomas was with them. Though the doors were locked, Jesus came and stood among them and said, 'Peace be with you!' Then he said to Thomas, 'Put your finger here; see my hands. Reach out your hand and put it into my side. Stop doubting and believe.' Thomas said to him, 'My Lord and my God!' Then Jesus told him, 'Because you have seen me, you have believed; blessed are those who have not seen and yet have believed.'" (John 20:26-29 NIV)

Once again, please note that the risen Christ supernaturally was able to enter through the walls of the house where the disciples were, even though the doors were locked. He went to Thomas and told him to stop doubting and to believe. Jesus also wants *you* to believe that *you* have been given a total, complete and absolute victory throughout your life on earth and when you die and go to heaven because of the price that He paid for you.

There is no question that the resurrected body of Jesus Christ still had the marks of the wounds that He suffered when He was crucified for you. He will bear the marks of His crucifixion throughout eternity. If Jesus is your Savior, you will live eternally with Him in heaven. You will see with your own eyes the enormous price that Jesus paid for you.

If Jesus Christ is your Savior and you have absolute faith in Him, you can be assured that the magnificent victory that He won has been passed on to you. "...these are written that you may believe that Jesus is the Christ, the Son of God, and that by believing you may have life in his name." (John 20:31 NIV)

The apostle Paul explained this great spiritual truth in his first letter to the Corinthians when he said, "Now, brothers, I want to remind you of the gospel I preached to you, which you received and on which you have taken your stand. By this gospel you are saved, if you hold firmly to the word I preached to you. Otherwise, you have believed in vain. For what I received I passed on to you as of first importance: that Christ died for our sins according to the Scriptures, that he was buried, that he was raised on the third day according to the Scriptures, and that he appeared to Peter, and then to the Twelve." (I Corinthians 15:1-5 NIV)

After revealing to Mary Magdalene and His disciples that He had risen from the dead, Jesus then openly revealed His resurrected body to many other people. "After that, he appeared to more than five hundred of the brothers at the same time, most of whom are still living, though some have fallen asleep. Then he appeared to James, then to all the apostles, and last of all he appeared to me also, as to one abnormally born." (I Corinthians 15:6-8 NIV)

Jesus gave His disciples instructions as to what He wanted them to do. The following words are called the Great Commission. "…He said to them, Go into all the world and preach and publish openly the good news (the Gospel) to every creature [of the whole human race]. He who believes [who adheres to and trusts in and relies on the Gospel and Him Whom it sets forth] and is baptized will be saved [from the penalty of eternal death]; but he who does not believe [who does not adhere to and trust in and rely on the Gospel and Him Whom it sets forth] will be condemned." (Mark 16:15-16 AMP)

Jesus instructed His followers then and He instructs *you* today to share the scriptural facts that you have read in the last four chapters with everyone you possibly can. God has commissioned you to spread the gospel so that each of these people will be given the opportunity to receive Jesus Christ as his or her Savior, to live joyfully throughout their lives on earth and to live eternally with Jesus in the glory of heaven.

Before Jesus ascended into heaven, He descended into hell where He won a total victory for you. The psalmist David prophesied that the Messiah would ascend into heaven with a complete victory. He said, "You have ascended on high. You have led away captive a train of vanquished foes…" (Psalm 68:18 AMP)

Please highlight or underline the words "a train of vanquished foes" in this verse of Scripture. These words refer to Satan and his demons. Satan and his demons were "vanquished." They were defeated by Jesus Christ Who won a total victory over them.

The apostle Paul in his letter to the Ephesians referred to this verse of Scripture when he said, "…When He ascended on high, He led captivity captive [He led a train of vanquished foes]…" (Ephesians 4:8 AMP)

How did Jesus win this victory? During the three days from the time He died on the cross and was raised from the dead and appeared to His followers, Jesus descended into hell *where He took your place.* "…Now what can this, He ascended, mean but that He had previously descended from [the heights of] heaven into [the depths], the lower parts of the earth? He Who descended is the [very] same as He Who also has ascended high above all the heavens…" (Ephesians 4:9-10 AMP)

Before Jesus "ascended" into heaven, He "descended" into hell. He took the keys of hell and death away from Satan. Jesus said, "…I am the First and the Last, and the Ever-living One [I am living in the eternity of the eternities]. I died, but see, I am alive forevermore; and I possess the keys of death and Hades (the realm of the dead)." (Revelation 1:17 AMP)

Jesus took the keys of hell away from Satan. He took the keys of death away from Satan. Jesus won a total victory for *you.* Once this was accomplished, His work on earth was finished. "After he said this, he was taken up before their very eyes, and a cloud hid him from their sight. They were looking intently up into the sky as he was going, when suddenly two men dressed in white stood beside them. 'Men of Galilee,' they said, 'why do you stand here looking into the sky? This same Jesus, who has been taken from you into heaven, will come back in the same way you have seen him go into heaven.'" (Acts 1:9-11 NIV)

The first four chapters of this book have been filled with facts from the holy Bible that clearly explain exactly what transpired from the time that the virgin Mary gave birth to Jesus Christ to the time that the victorious Christ rose from earth to return to heaven. We believe that we live in the last generation before Jesus Christ returns to earth. We believe that He will come back in the near future in the same way that He went to heaven.

If you have fully grasped the scriptural truths that have been explained in these last four chapters, your heart will be *filled with gratitude* to Jesus Christ for the enormous sacrifice that He made for you. You should thank Him and praise Him continually for the magnificent gift that He has given to *you*.

The remainder of this book is filled with facts from the holy Scriptures that will show you exactly what God instructs you to do to live in continual joy throughout the remainder of your life because of the magnificent victory that Jesus won for you.

Chapter 5

Your Heart Should Be Filled with Gratitude

The gruesome facts about the Garden of Gethsemane, the phony trials by Jewish and Roman officials and the scourging and crucifixion of Jesus Christ clearly show you the enormous price that Jesus paid for you. You owe everything you have and everything you are to Jesus. Is your heart filled with gratitude to Jesus?

Gratitude is essential to the joy of the Lord being manifested in your life. "Yet now has [Christ, the Messiah] reconciled [you to God] in the body of His flesh through death, in order to present you holy and faultless and irreproachable in His [the Father's] presence." (Colossians 1:22 AMP)

Jesus paid the price to "reconcile you to God." He became sin for you. He died on the cross for you "in order to present you holy and faultless and irreproachable" to His Father. Jesus "...was betrayed and put to death because of our misdeeds and was raised to secure our justification (our acquittal), [making our account balance and absolving us from all guilt before God]." (Romans 4:25 AMP)

Jesus died to pay the price for your misdeeds. Jesus was raised from the dead to give you acquittal from your sins. Jesus made your account balance and absolved you from *all* guilt before God." "...there is now no condemnation for those who are in Christ Jesus" (Romans 8:1 NIV)

Please highlight or underline the words "no condemnation" in this verse of Scripture. If Jesus Christ is your Savior, you are not condemned for sins that you have committed in the past. Every sin has been paid for because of the enormous price that Jesus paid at Calvary.

Your heart should be filled with gratitude if you truly understand that Jesus went to hell for *you*. During the three days between the time that He died on the cross at Calvary and rose from the dead, Jesus went to hell in *your* place. He paid the agonizing price that you should have to pay.

If you truly understand this magnificent spiritual truth, the words "Thank You, Jesus … Thank You, Jesus … Thank You, Jesus … Thank You, Jesus … Thank You, Jesus" will flow spontaneously out of your mouth throughout every day and night of your life.

The psalmist David said, "Blessed and happy and to be envied are those whose iniquities are forgiven and whose sins are covered up and completely buried. Blessed and happy and to be envied is the person of whose sin the Lord will take no account nor reckon it against him." (Romans 4:7-8 AMP)

If Jesus Christ is your Savior, *you* are "blessed" because all of your sins have been forgiven. *You* are blessed because God does not charge any of your sins against you. If you are absolutely certain that you will live eternally in the glory of heaven, your heart will be filled with joy.

Imagine that you were sentenced to life imprisonment and that you saw absolutely no way out of the predicament you faced. Imagine that suddenly the governor pardoned you and that you were set free from living in prison for the remainder of your life. Imagine how grateful you would feel.

This is *exactly* what happened when Jesus Christ paid the full price for all of your sins. If Jesus Christ truly is your Savior, your heart should sing with joy. The psalmist said, "The Lord has done great things for us! We are glad!" (Psalm 126:3 AMP)

This statement applies to all of the great things that God has done. It also applies to the price that Jesus paid on the cross at Calvary. You should be like the prophet Isaiah who said, "I will greatly rejoice in the Lord, my soul will exult in my God; for He has clothed me with the garments of salvation, He has covered me with the robe of righteousness, as a bridegroom decks himself with a garland, and as a bride adorns herself with her jewels." (Isaiah 61:10 AMP)

Isaiah was speaking prophetically here. You should "greatly rejoice in the Lord" because He has "clothed you with the garments of salvation." He has covered all of your sins with the righteousness that He has provided for you. "...the [uncompromisingly] righteous man sings and rejoices." (Proverbs 29:6 AMP)

Please highlight or underline the words "sings and rejoices" in this verse of Scripture. If Jesus Christ is your Savior, you are righteous before God. You should do your very best at all times to live a righteous life by consistently learning and obeying God's instructions (see Proverbs 4:13, James 1:22 and I Peter 1:14).

Part of living a righteous life of obedience is to constantly "sing and rejoice." You should be like the psalmist who said, "...You, O Lord, have made me glad by Your works; at the deeds of Your hands I joyfully sing." (Psalm 92:4 AMP)

Your heart should sing with joy because of the tremendous gratitude you have toward the Lord for everything He has done and is doing. The more you realize how unclean, vain and unrighteous you actually are, the more you will praise Jesus and thank Him for setting you free from all of your sin. You should be extremely grateful for the grace of God. Praise should well up from your heart continually.

If your heart is filled with gratitude for all that Jesus has done for you, you will not be able to stop praising Him and thanking Him. Whatever fills your heart to overflowing always will pour out of your mouth. Jesus said, "...out of the fullness (the overflow, the superabundance) of the heart the mouth speaks." (Matthew 12:34 AMP)

The overflowing gratitude in your heart should pour out of your mouth throughout every day and night of your life. Again and again you should spontaneously thank Jesus and praise Him.

God, through His beloved Son Jesus Christ, has provided many blessings that you do not deserve. He does not give you what you do deserve. "...thanks be to God for His Gift, [precious] beyond telling [His indescribable, inexpressible, free Gift]!" (II Corinthians 9:15 AMP)

Please highlight or underline the words "beyond telling," "indescribable" and "inexpressible" in this verse of Scripture and the amplification. The Gift of Jesus Christ is *so great* that you cannot describe it or put it into words.

Thank God for the precious Gift of Jesus Christ. Thank Jesus continually for the enormous price that He paid for you. "…you are a chosen people, a royal priesthood, a holy nation, a people belonging to God, that you may declare the praises of him who called you out of darkness into his wonderful light." (I Peter 2:9 NIV)

Please highlight or underline the words "declare the praises of him who called you out of darkness into his wonderful light" in this verse of Scripture. Praise Jesus continually for rescuing you from the darkness of Satan and the world and bringing you into His "wonderful light."

Know that you are a "chosen" person. God has been so good to you. You should be like Daniel who "…got down upon his knees three times a day and prayed and gave thanks before his God…" (Daniel 6:10 AMP)

Consistently giving thanks to God is an indication of spiritual maturity. Christians who thank the Lord and praise Him continually are mature, humble and grateful. This constant attitude of gratitude releases the joy of the Lord that is inside of you.

You should rejoice continually because you are absolutely certain that you are a member of the royal family of God, that God Himself is your loving Father and that you are His beloved child. "I will be a Father to you, and you will be my sons and daughters, says the Lord Almighty." (II Corinthians 6:18 NIV)

Refuse to give up your joy because of anything you may have done in your past. *Know* that God has given you a clean slate. Rejoice in this magnificent truth. Praise the Lord and thank Him continually.

A Christian whose heart is filled with gratitude is close to God. Ingratitude blocks you from drawing close to God. Your Father knows your heart. He knows whether you are truly grateful to Him. Thank God continually and draw closer and closer to Him.

Chapter 6

Rejoice Because You Will Live Eternally in Heaven

If Jesus Christ is your Savior, your life should revolve around your deep certainty that you will live eternally in heaven. Your heart should sing with joy because you are absolutely certain that you will live in this glorious and magnificent place throughout eternity. You must not give up your joy because of what happens or does not happen on earth. A mature eternal perspective will help you to keep your joy throughout your life on earth.

You should do your very best to serve the Lord here on earth and to successfully carry out every assignment He has given to you. If you do, you have a great deal to look forward to in heaven. Jesus said, "Be glad and supremely joyful, for your reward in heaven is great (strong and intense)…" (Matthew 5:12 AMP)

Jesus did not tell you just to be joyful. He instructed you to be "*supremely* joyful." Your heart will be filled with joy if you know that you will be greatly rewarded in heaven for your service to the Lord here on earth. "Set your minds on things above, not on earthly things." (Colossians 3:2 NIV)

Please highlight or underline the words "not on earthly things" in this verse of Scripture. These words include whatever problems you will face at any time during your life on earth. As difficult as these problems might seem, your Father has instructed you to "set your mind" on heaven, absolutely refusing to allow any problems on earth to steal the joy of the Lord from you.

Unbelievers and some Christians focus entirely on the 70, 80 or 90 years that they hope to live on earth. Your Father does *not* want you to focus on the relatively short time you will live on earth and to virtually ignore the endless trillions of years that you will live in heaven.

We use the words "trillions of years" only as a frame of reference. There are no years in heaven. However, the length of time that you will live in heaven compared to the relatively short period of time you will live on earth could be compared to one tiny grain of sand on the largest beach in the world. Rejoice continually because you are certain that your name is written in the Lamb's Book of Life and that you will live joyously throughout eternity in the glory of heaven.

Your home on earth is only temporary. Your real home is in heaven. When you arrive in heaven, you will have come home. "...we are citizens of the state (commonwealth, homeland) which is in heaven..." (Philippians 3:20 AMP)

If Jesus Christ is your Savior, you are in this world, not of this world. Look forward to going home. Instead of identifying with the world, identify with your glorious eternal home in heaven. Look forward to the magnificent day when you will enter into heaven to live in this marvelous place throughout eternity.

You cannot even begin to comprehend the magnificence of heaven. You have no frame of reference to understand the glory of heaven. Nothing you have ever seen or heard can remotely compare with the glory, beauty and magnificence of heaven.

Think of the most beautiful place you have ever been. Know that the beauty of heaven far exceeds the beauty of anything you have seen on earth. "...Eye hath not seen, nor ear heard, neither have entered into the heart of man, the things which God hath prepared for them that love him." (I Corinthians 2:9 KJV)

Heaven will be *much greater* than you can possibly comprehend, even if you meditate often on the glorious facts in the Bible pertaining to heaven. You should be very excited about heaven. *Release* the joy that you have in you because of the glorious eternal life that awaits you.

As you grow older, you are drawing closer and closer to living eternally in the glory of heaven. Some older people lose their joy because they realize that their remaining time on earth is limited. Christians should do *just the opposite*. Do not give up your joy if you know that your remaining time on earth is short. Instead, rejoice because you know that you are continually drawing closer to living eternally in the glory of heaven.

When you arrive in heaven every problem that you ever experienced on earth will have disappeared forever. "God will wipe away every tear from their eyes; and death shall be no more, neither shall there be anguish (sorrow and mourning) nor grief nor pain any more, for the old conditions and the former order of things have passed away." (Revelation 21:4 AMP)

Please highlight or underline the words "God will wipe away every tear from their eyes" in this verse of Scripture. No one in heaven experiences "anguish (sorrow and mourning) nor grief nor pain."

There are many unsavory people on earth, but everyone in heaven is completely pure. "...nothing that defiles or profanes or is unwashed shall ever enter it, nor anyone who commits abominations (unclean, detestable, morally repugnant things) or practices falsehood, but only those whose names are recorded in the Lamb's Book of Life." (Revelation 21:27 AMP)

You can be certain that people whose sins have not been cleansed by the blood of Jesus Christ will not live eternally in heaven because their names are not recorded in the Lamb's Book of Life. No one in heaven is proud or selfish. All of the misery that is caused by self-centeredness on earth will have disappeared.

No one in heaven is lonely. You will enjoy a glorious reunion in heaven with all of your Christian loved ones and friends who preceded you to heaven. All of the earthly imperfections that you have will be *instantly cleansed* when you arrive in heaven. The Bible explains this magnificent truth when it speaks of "the spirits of just men made perfect." (Hebrews 12:23 KJV)

You will live throughout eternity in heaven with your humble and loving brothers and sisters in the Lord. You will enjoy glorious eternal rest in heaven. "...Blessed are the dead which die in the Lord from henceforth: Yea, saith the Spirit, that they may rest from their labours; and their works do follow them." (Revelation 14:13 KJV)

You have so much to look forward to in heaven. If Jesus Christ is your Savior, He has prepared a beautiful home for you in heaven. Jesus said, "In My Father's house there are many dwelling places (homes). If it were not so, I would have told you; for I am going away to prepare a place for you." (John 14:2 AMP)

Please highlight or underline the words "I am going away to prepare a place for you" in this verse of Scripture. Know that Jesus Christ has personally supervised the construction of a beautiful home for *you* in heaven where you will live throughout eternity. *Rejoice* because you are certain of this great truth.

Every question you have ever had will be answered in heaven. "Now we see but a poor reflection as in a mirror; then we shall see face to face. Now I know in part; then I shall know fully, even as I am fully known." (I Corinthians 13:12 NIV)

No one in heaven has a tired and aching body. Every person in heaven is healthy, vibrant and happy. If you are growing older and you have some physical ailments, you can be certain that your loving Father will give you a glorious new body that is completely healthy. "...we know that if the earthly tent we live in is destroyed, we have a building from God, an eternal house in heaven, not built by human hands. Meanwhile we groan, longing to be clothed with our heavenly dwelling" (II Corinthians 5:1-2 NIV)

The Bible refers to your earthly body as a "tent." A tent is a temporary dwelling place. Your present body was designed for life on earth which is a temporary dwelling place. Your earthly body will be destroyed when you die. God has a permanent new body for you in heaven. Any sickness in your body will *not* go with you to heaven.

There is no darkness in heaven. Night does not exist. There are no cloudy or stormy days. There is no need for the sun or the moon because the glory of God will illuminate heaven at all times.

Heaven glows with the radiance of God. You will be continually aware of this glorious luminous light from the moment you arrive in heaven. "There will be no more night. They will not need the light of

a lamp or the light of the sun, for the Lord God will give them light...."
(Revelation 22:5 NIV)

You will constantly sing with joy when you are in heaven. "...the ransomed of the LORD will return. They will enter Zion with singing; everlasting joy will crown their heads. Gladness and joy will overtake them, and sorrow and sighing will flee away." (Isaiah 35:10 NIV)

Zion is a hill outside of Jerusalem, but the word Zion also is used in the Bible to refer to heaven. When you enter into heaven, you will come in singing. You will begin an eternal life of everlasting joy.

Everyone in heaven is filled with joy. No one in heaven is anxious, worried or discouraged. There are no negative emotions in heaven. Rejoice continually now because you are absolutely certain that *you* will live in the glory of heaven throughout eternity.

The remainder of this book contains many facts from the holy Scriptures pertaining to praising the Lord. You should develop the habit of praising the Lord here on earth because you *will* be praising Him throughout eternity in heaven.

When the apostle John was supernaturally transported to heaven, he reported that everyone in heaven praises the Lord loudly. John said, "...I heard what sounded like a mighty shout of a great crowd in heaven, exclaiming, Hallelujah (praise the Lord)! Salvation and glory (splendor and majesty) and power (dominion and authority) [belong] to our God!" (Revelation 19:1 AMP)

John heard a voice coming from the throne of God telling every person in heaven to praise God and to revere Him. "Then from the throne there came a voice, saying, Praise our God, all you servants of His, you who reverence Him, both small and great!" (Revelation 19:5 AMP)

The word "all" in this verse of Scripture includes *you*. The praise in heaven is so loud that John compared it to the roar of thunder. He said, "...I heard what sounded like the shout of a vast throng, like the boom of many pounding waves, and like the roar of terrific and mighty peals of thunder, exclaiming, Hallelujah (praise the Lord)!..." (Revelation 19:6 AMP)

You should especially rejoice because of your certainty that you will not live eternally in hell. If you do not know what the Bible says about living eternally in heaven or hell, we recommend our books titled *What Will Heaven Be Like?* and *What Does God Say?*. These books contain many scriptural *facts* pertaining to heaven and hell.

Rejoice because you are certain that you have been completely forgiven for every sin you have ever committed. Rejoice continually because you are absolutely certain that you will be *going home* to live with Jesus throughout eternity. Rejoice because you are certain that you will be healthy and happy throughout eternity in heaven.

Chapter 7

Rejoice in the Victory
That Jesus Christ Won for You

In this chapter we will compare the joy of the Lord to the happiness of the world. The joy of the Lord is much deeper than the happiness of the world. People in the world are happy depending on the circumstances in their lives. The joy of the Lord is completely independent of circumstances. The joy of the Lord comes from a close and intimate relationship with God, a heart that is filled with the Word of God and absolute trust in God.

People in the world are happy when their finances are good, when the weather is the way they want it to be, when their favorite team wins the ball game and, in general, when everything is going well in their lives. Many people in the world are unhappy when they have problems with their health, their finances or their families. Sometimes they are unhappy because the weather prevents them from doing what they want to do, because they need expensive automobile repairs or because of traffic congestion.

Will you have absolute faith in God or will you allow your joy to be dictated by the circumstances you face? Unfortunately, some Christians believe in the power of the problems they face more than they believe in the power of God. They may not open their mouths and admit this, but their words and actions in the face of adversity show that they believe more in the power of the adversity they face than they do in the power of God.

The world's happiness is temporary and externally oriented because it is based on external conditions. Christian joy is permanent and internally oriented because it comes from a close and intimate relationship with Jesus Christ and constant awareness of the victory that Jesus Christ has won for *you*.

You often cannot control the circumstances in your life, but you *can* control your *reaction* to these circumstances. If you faithfully obey your Father's instructions to renew your mind in His Word each day and to meditate day and night on the holy Scriptures, you will consistently be programming yourself with the supernatural living Word of God. You will react to the circumstances you face based on the instructions and promises in God's Word instead of allowing your emotions to control your life.

Many Christians do *not* study the Bible each day to renew their minds in God's Word. Many Christians do *not* obey their Father's instructions to meditate day and night on His Word. As a result, their lives are primarily lived as a reaction to the circumstances they face.

God has given freedom of choice to each person He has created. You continually choose how you will react to the circumstances you face. Your *heart* is the key to your life. "Keep and guard your heart with all vigilance and above all that you guard, for out of it flow the springs of life." (Proverbs 4:23 AMP)

Please highlight or underline the words "guard your heart with all vigilance" in this verse of Scripture. If you have faithfully obeyed your Father's instructions to renew your mind in His Word each day, your *mind* will be filled with the Word of God. When you consistently meditate on the Word of God, God's Word drops from your mind into your *heart*.

If you faithfully obey your Father's instructions to meditate day and night on His Word, your heart will be filled with joy because your heart will be filled with God's supernatural living Word. "...he who has a glad heart has a continual feast [regardless of circumstances]." (Proverbs 15:15 AMP)

Please highlight or underline the words "regardless of circumstances" in the amplification of this verse of Scripture. If you have "a glad heart" that is filled with God's Word, you will *not* be overcome by the circumstances you face.

Your Father does not want you to allow the problems you face to overcome you. He wants you to rejoice continually because your heart is filled with His Word and because you are certain that He has given you victory over every circumstance in your life.

Jesus Christ left heaven and came to earth to win a magnificent victory that is greater than any victory that has ever been won. You should rejoice in your confidence that this victory applies to *you*.

Refuse to allow the problems you face to intimidate you. Refuse to give up your joy. Rejoice in your certainty that the victorious Jesus Christ lives in your heart.

God never intended for you to only be happy when everything is going well in your life. God created you to live in His joy at all times, regardless of the circumstances you face. "In the day of prosperity be joyful, but in the day of adversity consider that God has made the one side by side with the other..." (Ecclesiastes 7:14 AMP)

Most people in the world are "joyful in the day of prosperity." Your Father wants you to be joyful "in the day of adversity" as well. He wants you to be absolutely certain that He will bring you safely through whatever adversity you face. Jesus said, "...In the world you have tribulation and trials and distress and frustration; but be of good cheer [take courage; be confident, certain, undaunted]! For I have overcome the world. [I have deprived it of power to harm you and have conquered it for you.]" (John 16:33 AMP)

Please highlight or underline the words "be of good cheer" in this verse of Scripture. Do *not* allow the problems you face to pull you down, no matter how severe these problems may seem. Trust completely in Jesus to bring you safely through all adversity. Rejoice in the magnificent victory that Jesus has won for *you*. If you *really believe* that Jesus Christ has "overcome the world," you *will* rejoice in the face of adversity.

Please highlight or underline the words "take courage; be confident, certain, undaunted" in the amplification of this verse of Scripture. Your confidence in Jesus Christ should give you the certainty that you must have so that you will persevere in faith when you face adversity.

Please highlight or underline the words "I have overcome the world" in this verse of Scripture. Jesus Christ *has overcome* every problem you have ever faced, every problem you face now and every problem you will face.

Please highlight or underline the words "I have deprived it of power to harm *you* and have conquered it for *you*" in the amplification of this verse of Scripture. You will "be of good cheer" at all times if you are *absolutely certain* that Jesus Christ has given you victory over every problem you will ever face.

You are not fighting for a victory. You are fighting *from* a victory. Jesus already has won the battle for you. You should thank God and praise Him continually for the victory you have been given by Jesus Christ. "...thanks be to God, Who in Christ always leads us in triumph [as trophies of Christ's victory]..." (II Corinthians 2:14 AMP)

Please highlight or underline the words "always leads us in triumph" in this verse of Scripture. God does not say that He will lead you in triumph sometimes or most of the time. He says that He will *always* lead you in triumph.

The victory of Jesus Christ is total, complete and unchallenged in the spiritual realm. Focus consistently on these *facts* from God's Word about the supernatural victory that has been given to *you*. Praise Jesus. Thank Him continually for the victory that you know is yours.

You must understand that God always is in complete control, whether it looks that way or not. Rejoice because you know that you have been give absolute victory through Jesus Christ. "The Lord reigns, let the earth rejoice..." (Psalm 97:1 AMP)

When this verse of Scripture says "let the earth rejoice," these words refer to *you*. You should rejoice at all times because of your absolute certainty that God "reigns." *Know* that He is in complete control over everything that is taking place on earth. We should "...hold fast and firm to the end our joyful and exultant confidence and sense of triumph in our hope [in Christ]." (Hebrews 3:6 AMP)

Please highlight or underline the words "joyful and exultant confidence" in this verse of Scripture. If you have a deep inner "sense of triumph" because you have faithfully meditated on these *facts* from the holy Scriptures pertaining to the victory that Jesus Christ won for *you*, you will "hold fast and firm to the end." You will never give up (see our book titled *Never, Never Give Up*).

You should *always* rejoice because of Who Jesus Christ is and because of your absolute certainty pertaining to the magnificent victory He has won for you. Rejoice continually just as you would rejoice if this victory already has been brought into manifestation in your life. You do not have to wait to see the manifestation of the victory of Jesus Christ to rejoice. God's Word says that you have this victory. Rejoice and keep on rejoicing.

You must not allow Satan and his demons to steal the victory that Jesus won for you. If your mind and your heart are filled with God's promises pertaining to this victory, you will not give up your joy, no matter what circumstances you face.

Satan's demons want you to be sad and melancholy when you face adversity. They will do everything they can to put negative thoughts into your mind. "...that enemy of yours, the devil, roams around like a lion roaring [in fierce hunger], seeking someone to seize upon and devour. Withstand him; be firm in faith [against his onset – rooted, established, strong, immovable, and determined]..." (I Peter 5:8-9 AMP)

Satan is your "enemy." He wants to "devour" you. You are instructed to "withstand him" because you have deeply rooted faith in Jesus Christ and the victory He won for you. Your Father wants your heart to be filled with joy because you are certain that the victory of Jesus Christ will be manifested in your life. Open your mouth and praise the Lord continually. Continually speak the Word of God pertaining to the victory that Jesus Christ won for you.

Chapter 8

Enjoy an Intimate Relationship with the Lord

In the last chapter you saw several verses of Scripture that explain the relationship between the joy of the Lord and your faith in the Lord. In this chapter you will see what the Bible says about a close and intimate relationship with the Lord and receiving the joy of the Lord in your life. "Come close to God and He will come close to you..." (James 4:8 AMP)

Please highlight or underline the words "He *will* come close to you" in this verse of Scripture. Think of the enormity of this statement. *God Himself* promises to come close to *you*. However, you must consistently initiate the relationship. *If* you come close to God, your Father promises that He *will* come close to you.

As you continually draw closer to God and develop a deep and intimate relationship with Him, His joy will fill your heart. Nothing will be able to steal His joy from you because the intimacy and closeness of your relationship with Him will be much more powerful than any adversity you will ever face.

Your Father wants to have a close and intimate relationship with you. You will enjoy this close and intimate relationship if you are very serious about drawing close to God and if you follow the specific instructions your Father has given to you in His Word.

There is a direct relationship between the constancy of joy in your life and the closeness and intimacy of your relationship with the Lord.

Mature Christians who walk closely with the Lord do not give up their joy. They trust the Lord completely at all times, regardless of the circumstances they face.

Unbelievers know nothing of the joy of the Lord. Religious people who attend church regularly but do not set aside time to draw closer to the Lord do not experience the joy of the Lord. If you spend quiet time in close and intimate fellowship with the Lord each day, you *will* experience His joy in your life.

Jesus Christ paid an enormous price so that you can experience a close relationship with God. "...it is through Him that we both [whether far off or near] now have an introduction (access) by one [Holy] Spirit to the Father [so that we are able to approach Him]." (Ephesians 2:18 AMP)

Please highlight or underline the words "through Him" in this verse of Scripture. Jesus Christ has given you "an introduction to the Father." You are able to approach Him through the Holy Spirit. You, with all of your faults and shortcomings, have been given the opportunity to develop a close relationship with God. "...because of our faith in Him, we dare to have the boldness (courage and confidence) of free access (an unreserved approach to God with freedom and without fear)." (Ephesians 3:12 AMP)

Please highlight or underline the words "because of our faith in Him" in this verse of Scripture. *Do you* have absolute faith in Jesus Christ? *Do you* have the "boldness" to approach God "with freedom and without fear" because you know that Jesus Christ has made it possible for you to draw close to God? If you really believe that you have been given the privilege of drawing close to God, your heart will overflow with joy because you are certain that God Himself desires to have a close relationship with you.

Your relationship with God should not be a Sunday morning relationship or a two or three times a week relationship when you attend church. Your relationship with God should be close and intimate throughout every day and night of your life. Every aspect of your life should revolve around your certainty of God's indwelling presence and His desire to have a close relationship with you.

There is a direct relationship between the intimacy of your relationship with Jesus Christ and experiencing His supernatural joy. "Without having seen Him, you love Him; though you do not [even] now see Him, you believe in Him and exult and thrill with inexpressible and glorious (triumphant, heavenly) joy." (I Peter 1:8 AMP)

You have never seen Jesus with your natural eyesight, but you should love Him wholeheartedly even though you cannot see Him. You should spend so much quiet time alone with Him each day that you develop a close and intimate relationship with Him.

Please highlight or underline the words "glorious (triumphant, heavenly) joy" in this verse of Scripture and the amplification. If your relationship with Jesus Christ is close and intimate, your heart will sing with supernatural joy that is comparable to the joy you will experience when you are in heaven. "...let the hearts of those rejoice who seek and require the Lord [as their indispensable necessity]." (Psalm 105:3 AMP)

Please highlight or underline the words "indispensable necessity" in the amplification of this verse of Scripture. A close relationship with the Lord is not a nice to have – this close relationship is a have to have. If you truly are close to the Lord, you will rejoice continually, regardless of the circumstances you face, because His joy will flood your heart. "...you will seek Me, inquire for, and require Me [as a vital necessity] and find Me when you search for Me with all your heart." (Jeremiah 29:13 AMP)

Please highlight or underline the words "a vital necessity" in the amplification of this verse of Scripture. A close and intimate relationship with the Lord is important at all times and will be even more important during the difficult times that are coming upon the world. Make the commitment now, if you have not already, that you will search for a close relationship with the Lord "with all your heart."

You must be absolutely certain that Jesus Christ Who won such a glorious victory when He rose from the dead lives in your heart if you have asked Him to be your Savior. Jesus said, "...apart from Me [cut off from vital union with Me] you can do nothing." (John 15:5 AMP)

The words "vital union" in this verse of Scripture are extremely important. You have seen the words "indispensable necessity," "vital necessity" and "vital union" in the last three verses of Scripture. There is no question that a close relationship with the Lord is *vitally* important to *you*. "Blessed (happy, fortunate, to be envied) are they who keep His testimonies, and who seek, inquire for and of Him and crave Him with the whole heart." (Psalm 119:2 AMP)

Do you sincerely desire to be "blessed, happy and fortunate?" You will experience these wonderful attributes if you consistently learn and obey the instructions in God's Word and if you seek God "and crave Him with the whole heart." Nothing should be more important to you than to continually draw closer to the Lord.

When God created you, He created a void in your heart that can only be filled by a close and intimate relationship with Him. Many people are aware of this void and they go to great extremes pursuing many things in the world in a vain attempt to fill this void. You must understand that *only God* can satisfy this deep inner longing. You should be like the psalmist who said, "My inner self thirsts for God, for the living God...." (Psalm 42:2 AMP)

Do you hunger and thirst for an intimate relationship with God? Everything in your life should revolve around your certainty of God's desire for a close and intimate relationship with you. *Know* that God lives in your heart and that He is with you throughout every day of your life. Every aspect of your life should be centered around your absolute certainty of God's indwelling presence. "...He is not far from each one of us. For in Him we live and move and have our being..." (Acts 17:27-28 AMP)

Please highlight or underline the words "each one of us" in this passage of Scripture. These words apply to *you*. Your Father wants every aspect of your life to revolve around the magnificence of His indwelling presence. He wants you to "live and move and have your being" based upon the intimacy of your relationship with Him. Jesus said, "...whoever loses his [lower] life on My account will find it [the higher life]." (Matthew 10:39 AMP)

Jesus instructs you to turn away from the "lower life." These words refer to focusing on the things of the world. Jesus does not want you to be preoccupied with worldly goals. Instead, He wants you to continually draw closer to Him. As your relationship with Jesus becomes more intimate, you will "find the higher life." His joy will well up within you.

You should rejoice because you are absolutely certain that the Lord desires a close and intimate relationship with *you*. "...let him who glories glory in this: that he understands and knows Me [personally and practically, directly discerning and recognizing My character], that I am the Lord, Who practices loving-kindness, judgment, and righteousness in the earth, for in these things I delight, says the Lord." (Jeremiah 9:24 AMP)

Please highlight or underline the words "personally and practically" in the amplification of this verse of Scripture. Your relationship with the Lord should not be general and theoretical – it should be personal and practical.

Christians who enjoy a close and intimate relationship with the Lord are never lonely. They rejoice continually in the intimacy of their relationship with the Lord. Everything in their lives comes from the inside out, not from the outside in.

The Lord wants to give you meaning, satisfaction and fulfillment in your life. If you have a deep and sincere desire for a close relationship with Him, your desires and His desires for you will be one and the same. "Delight yourself also in the Lord, and He will give you the desires and secret petitions of your heart." (Psalm 37:4 AMP)

When you "delight yourself" in the Lord, you receive great pleasure and joy from your relationship with Him. Nothing is more important to you than this wonderful relationship.

Please highlight or underline the words "He will give you the desires and secret petitions of your heart" in this verse of Scripture. The Lord knows every minute detail about you (see Psalm 139:1-4 and Hebrews 4:13). *If* you delight in Him and continually draw closer to Him, He *will* give you your secret desires that you may not even have been able to verbalize.

You should have a constant consciousness of the indwelling presence of the Lord. Speak to Him throughout each day. He wants to be your closest friend. He wants you to know that He is with you at all times and that He will help you (see Isaiah 41:13).

He wants every aspect of your life to revolve around the intimacy of your relationship with Him. The happiness of the world comes and goes. The joy of the Lord will be constant in your life if you stay close to Him throughout each day of your life.

This chapter is filled with facts from the holy Scriptures regarding a closer and more intimate relationship with the Lord. If you study and meditate on these scriptural instructions and faithfully obey these instructions, you *will* consistently experience the joy of the Lord in your life.

Chapter 9

The Joy of the Lord Is within You

You have learned that God does not want you to allow the circumstances you face to steal His joy from you. You have learned that Jesus Christ has given you a tremendous victory over every problem you will ever face. In this chapter you will learn facts from the holy Scriptures that will clearly show you that the joy of the Lord is *within you* if you have turned from your sin and received Jesus Christ as your Savior.

People in the world look for happiness from external sources. They pursue pleasure. They go here and go there and do this and do that. *Why* would you ever pursue something that you already have? If you are certain that God's joy is inside of you, you will not go here, there and everywhere looking for what you already have.

The happiness of the world comes from the outside in. The joy of the Lord comes from the inside out. We are not saying that you should never enjoy hobbies or any wholesome pleasure. However, we are saying that you should not look for lasting joy from any external sources.

The happiness that unbelievers pursue actually is a yearning for the joy of the Lord. Jesus said, "…I say these things while I am still in the world, so that My joy may be made full and complete and perfect in them [that they may experience My delight fulfilled in them, that My enjoyment may be perfected in their own souls, that they may have My gladness within them, filling their hearts]." (John 17:13 AMP)

Please highlight or underline the words "so that My joy may be made full and complete and perfect *in them*" in this verse of Scripture. These words that Jesus spoke to His disciples shortly before He was crucified also apply to *you*. If Jesus Christ is your Savior, *you have been given His joy*. Jesus wants His joy to be perfected in your life. He wants your heart to be filled to overflowing with His supernatural joy that He has given to you.

Jesus told you *exactly* what you should do to receive His supernatural joy. He said, "He who believes in Me [who cleaves to and trusts in and relies on Me] as the Scripture has said, From his innermost being shall flow [continuously] springs and rivers of living water." (John 7:38 AMP)

Please highlight or underline the words "believes in Me" and "cleaves to and trusts in and relies on Me" in this verse of Scripture and the amplification. If you have a close and intimate relationship with Jesus and if you trust Him completely, "springs and rivers of living water" will flow from the Holy Spirit Who lives in your heart. The psalmist David knew that the joy of the Lord was in his heart. He said, "Thou hast put gladness in my heart..." (Psalm 4:7 KJV)

Please highlight or underline the words "gladness in my heart" in this verse of Scripture. Receive by faith the joy of the Lord that has been put into *your* heart if Jesus Christ is your Savior. The prophet Isaiah said, "Behold, God, my salvation! I will trust and not be afraid, for the Lord God is my strength and song; yes, He has become my salvation. Therefore with joy will you draw water from the wells of salvation." (Isaiah 12:2-3 AMP)

The joy of the Lord that Isaiah prophesied about in regard to salvation was made available to every person when Jesus Christ paid the full price for all of our sins on the cross at Calvary. Please highlight or underline the words "I will trust and not be afraid" in this passage of Scripture. Trust Jesus completely. Refuse to give in to adversity. Jesus has given you His strength (see Philippians 4:13). He has given you His joy.

The joy of the Lord is exuberant. It is deep and quiet. You can see the joy of the Lord in the eyes of believers who have it. It dances and sparkles like nothing else on earth.

Know that the joy of the Lord is inside of you. If Jesus Christ is your Savior, He lives in your heart. He is love. He is joy. Do not block His joy from being manifested in your life by fear, worry, doubt or any other negative emotion.

Adam and Eve were filled with joy before they sinned against God. Satan was able to steal their joy when they sinned. Jesus Christ redeemed this joy for *you*. He said, "…I came that they may have and enjoy life, and have it in abundance (to the full, till it overflows)." (John 10:10 AMP)

Please highlight or underline the words "enjoy life" in this verse of Scripture. *Jesus wants you to enjoy your life abundantly.* Please highlight or underline the words "to the full, till it overflows" in the amplification of this verse of Scripture. These words describe the magnitude of the abundant joy that Jesus has provided for *you* by the enormous victory that He won at Calvary.

Jesus paid a tremendous price so that *you* will be able to enjoy an abundance of joy. Jesus did not die on the cross for you to experience occasional joy. He wants your joy to be full and overflowing. He wants you to enjoy life in abundance regardless of the circumstances you face.

So far, we have only looked at the portion of John 10:10 that explains the abundance of the joy that Jesus has provided for you. Now we will look at the entire verse of Scripture to see what Satan wants to do to you. Jesus said, "The thief comes only in order to steal and kill and destroy. I came that they may have and enjoy life, and have it in abundance (to the full, till it overflows)." (John 10:10 AMP)

The words "the thief" in this verse of Scripture refer to Satan and his demons. Satan and his demons want to "steal" everything they can that Jesus has provided for you. Satan and his demons want to "kill and destroy" you. Jesus wants you to enjoy your life in abundance.

You decide throughout every day of your life whether you will allow Satan and his demons to steal the joy of the Lord from you. You continually make this decision by the thoughts that you think in your mind, what you deeply believe in your heart, the words that you express with your mouth and the actions that you take. If your thoughts, the faith in your heart, your words and your actions are solidly anchored upon the Word of God in you and Jesus Christ Who lives in your heart, Satan will *not* be able to steal your joy or anything else from you.

You must not make the mistake of looking for joy from any external source. You must not do what people in the world do as they constantly pursue happiness from worldly sources. Jesus said, "…The kingdom of God does not come with signs to be observed or with visible display" (Luke 17:20 AMP)

Please highlight or underline the words "signs to be observed or with visible display" in this verse of Scripture. Do not look for joy from external sources. Joy and all of the other blessings that Jesus has provided for you come from deep down inside of yourself. Jesus went on to say, "…the kingdom of God is within you [in your hearts]…" (Luke 17:21 AMP)

God has placed *everything* you will ever need inside you. The joy of the Lord and everything else you will need from the kingdom of God *already is in your heart* if Jesus Christ is your personal Savior.

The joy of the Lord is not a surface joy that comes from having a superficial smile on your face. The joy of the Lord comes from deep down inside of you. It rises up whenever you face seemingly severe problems. The joy of the Lord is with you twenty-four hours a day throughout every day of your life. Every place you go, the joy of the Lord goes with you. You already have all of the joy you will ever need.

We now are ready to look into God's Word to learn additional facts that will assure you that God your Father lives in your heart, that Jesus Christ lives in your heart and that the Holy Spirit lives in your heart. You *will* experience the joy of the Lord if you have a continual consciousness of the indwelling presence of God and if your life is surrendered to God Who lives in your heart.

Chapter 10

Rejoice Because
God Is Always with You

You saw in the last chapter that the kingdom of God is within you if you have made the decision to receive Jesus Christ as your Savior. You learned that everything you will ever need was placed inside of you when you received Jesus Christ as your Savior. Christians do not need to look to the things of the world for joy, meaning and fulfillment in their lives.

When you face adversity, your Father wants your heart to sing with joy because you are absolutely certain that He is with you at all times and that He is in complete control. "The Lord your God is in the midst of you, a Mighty One, a Savior [Who saves]! He will rejoice over you with joy…" (Zephaniah 3:17 AMP)

Please highlight or underline the words "is in the midst of you" in this verse of Scripture. God is *not* far away. He is with you constantly. He is "a Mighty One." His power is more than sufficient, regardless of the seeming severity of any problem you face. He has provided glorious eternal salvation for you.

Your Father expresses joy because you are His beloved child. He "rejoices over *you* with joy." He wants you to rejoice also because you are absolutely certain that He is with you at all times and that His mighty power is more than sufficient to overcome any adversity you will face.

Jesus Christ is with you at all times. You should be like the apostle Paul who said, "I have been crucified with Christ [in Him I have shared His crucifixion]; it is no longer I who live, but Christ (the Messiah) lives in me; and the life I now live in the body I live by faith in (by adherence to and reliance on and complete trust in) the Son of God, Who loved me and gave Himself up for me." (Galatians 2:20 AMP)

Please highlight or underline the words "I have been crucified with Christ [in Him I have shared His crucifixion]" in this verse of Scripture and the amplification. Yield control of your life to Jesus Christ Who lives within you. Get out of the driver's seat. Die to yourself. Give up your desire to control your life. Allow Jesus Christ to live His life in you and through you.

Please highlight or underline the words "(by adherence to and reliance on and complete trust in) the Son of God, Who loved me and gave Himself up for me" in this verse of Scripture and the amplification. You should have absolute faith in Jesus Christ.

You should consistently study His instructions and do your very best to adhere to these instructions. You should rely on Him at all times because you trust Him completely. Praise Him and thank Him continually for Who He is and for the magnificent victory He has given to you.

You saw in Zephaniah 3:17 that God is with you at all times. You saw in Galatians 2:20 that Jesus Christ is with you at all times. You also can be absolutely certain that God's Holy Spirit is with you constantly. "…God's Spirit has His permanent dwelling in you…" (I Corinthians 3:16 AMP)

Please highlight or underline the words "permanent dwelling" in this verse of Scripture. *Know* that the Holy Spirit is always with you. He will never leave you. You should be consistently conscious of His indwelling presence. Rejoice that the mighty Holy Spirit lives in *your* heart.

If Jesus Christ is your Savior, God the Father, God the Son and God the Holy Spirit live in *your* heart. Your heart will sing with joy if you are constantly aware of the enormous spiritual power that resides within you. "…you are in Him, made full and having come to fullness of life [in Christ you too are filled with the Godhead – Father, Son and Holy Spirit – and reach full spiritual stature]...." (Colossians 2:10 AMP)

Please highlight or underline the words "the Godhead – Father, Son and Holy Spirit" in the amplification of this verse of Scripture. *You* are filled with the Godhead. *You* "reach full spiritual stature" because you are filled with the Godhead. "...Be not afraid, neither be dismayed, for the Lord your God is with you wherever you go." (Joshua 1:9 AMP)

These words that God spoke to Joshua when he became the leader of Israel apply to *you* today. Refuse to give in to fear because you are absolutely certain that Almighty God *is with you* wherever you go. "God is our Refuge and Strength [mighty and impenetrable to temptation], a very present and well-proved help in trouble. Therefore we will not fear, though the earth should change and though the mountains be shaken into the midst of the seas, though its waters roar and foam, though the mountains tremble at its swelling and tumult..." (Psalm 46:1-3 AMP)

Please highlight or underline the words "a very present and well-proved help in trouble" in this passage of Scripture. God is with you. He is proven. He knows exactly what to do when you face adversity. He does not want you to be afraid, regardless of what is happening in your life.

When you read about mountains being shaken into the roaring sea and mountains trembling, these words refer to severe problems. Do not be afraid. Rejoice continually because you are absolutely certain that God is with you at all times. "...I the Lord your God hold your right hand; I am the Lord, Who says to you, Fear not; I will help you!" (Isaiah 41:13 AMP)

Little children are secure when they are holding tightly onto the hand of their loving mother or father. Your Father holds *your* hand in the spiritual realm. He does not want you to be afraid. He wants you to be absolutely certain that He "*will* help you."

You saw in Galatians 2:20 that Jesus Christ is with you at all times. Jesus said, "Peace I leave with you; My [own] peace I now give and bequeath to you. Not as the world gives do I give to you. Do not let your hearts be troubled, neither let them be afraid. [Stop allowing yourselves to be agitated and disturbed; and do not permit yourselves to be fearful and intimidated and cowardly and unsettled.]" (John 14:27 AMP)

Please highlight or underline the words "My [own] peace I now give and bequeath to you" in this verse of Scripture and the amplification. If Jesus is your Savior, these words that He spoke to His disciples shortly before His crucifixion apply to you today. *Know* that Jesus has given His supernatural peace to *you*.

Please highlight or underline the two times the word "let" and the words "allowing" and "permit" are used in this verse of Scripture and the amplification. *You decide* whether you will allow fear to obtain a foothold in your life. Jesus said that you should *not* do this because He has given His supernatural peace to you.

Your Father has assured you that He will never let you down. "…He [God] Himself has said, I will not in any way fail you nor give you up nor leave you without support. [I will] not, [I will] not, [I will] not in any degree leave you helpless nor forsake nor let [you] down (relax My hold on you)! [Assuredly not!]" (Hebrews 13:5 AMP)

Please highlight or underline the words "I will not in any way fail you nor give you up nor leave you without support" in this verse of Scripture. This great truth is emphasized when the words "I will not" are repeated *four times* in this verse of Scripture and the amplification. Your loving Father has assured you that He will never leave you.

Your heart should overflow with joy because you are absolutely certain that God is always with you. "…we take comfort and are encouraged and confidently and boldly say, The Lord is my Helper; I will not be seized with alarm [I will not fear or dread or be terrified]…" (Hebrews 13:6 AMP)

Please highlight or underline the words "The Lord is my Helper. I will not be seized with alarm" in this verse of Scripture. Refuse to give in to fear because of your certainty that the Lord will help you. "…The beloved of the Lord shall dwell in safety by Him; He covers him all the day long, and makes His dwelling between his shoulders." (Deuteronomy 33:12 AMP)

You are "the beloved of the Lord." Your loving Father will keep you safe when you trust Him completely. He lives in your heart. He covers *you* "all the day long." "Fear not [there is nothing to fear], for I am with you; do not look around you in terror and be dismayed, for I am your God. I will strengthen and harden you to difficulties, yes, I will help you; yes, I will hold you up and retain you with My [victorious] right hand of rightness and justice." (Isaiah 41:10 AMP)

Please highlight or underline the words "there is nothing to fear" in the amplification of this verse of Scripture. The word "nothing" includes whatever problem you face at this time. Please highlight or underline the words "I will strengthen and harden you to difficulties." God *will* give you the strength that you need to overcome whatever problems you face.

Please highlight or underline the words "I will help you" in this verse of Scripture. Rejoice because your loving Father has repeatedly assured you that He will help you. "When thou passest through the waters, I will be with thee; and through the rivers, they shall not overflow thee: when thou walkest through the fire, thou shalt not be burned; neither shall the flame kindle upon thee. For I am the LORD thy God, the Holy One of Israel, thy Saviour..." (Isaiah 43:2-3 KJV)

Please highlight or underline the three times that the word "through" is used in this passage of Scripture. Meditate on this vitally important word. *Know* that your loving Father *will* bring you safely *through* all adversity that you will ever face *if* you will persevere in your deep, strong and unwavering faith in Him, absolutely refusing to give up.

Your Father repeatedly promises to watch over you and protect you. The Bible speaks of "...joy for the upright in heart [the irrepressible joy which comes from consciousness of His favor and protection]." (Psalm 97:11 AMP)

Rejoice in the face of adversity because you are continually conscious of your Father's favor and protection. If your heart sings with joy because of these great truths from God's holy Bible, you will be enthusiastic. The word "enthusiasm" comes from two Greek words "en" and "theos." The word "en" means "in." The word "theos" means "God." This word is the root of the English word "theology."

Some religious people think that God is far away. The Bible teaches that God is *not* far away from you. "Am I a God at hand, saith the LORD, and not a God afar off?" (Jeremiah 23:23 KJV)

If you face severe problems, you should focus continually on the scriptural facts in this chapter that assure you that God is with you at *all* times. You can be certain that He will help you. Rejoice continually. Praise God and thank Him in the face of adversity because He has promised that He *is* with you and that He *will* help you.

Chapter 11

God's Word Will Fill Your Heart with Joy

You have learned many scriptural facts about the relationship between trusting the Lord, a close and intimate relationship with the Lord and the joy of the Lord. The remainder of this book will be filled with many specific instructions telling you exactly what to do to experience the joy of the Lord. In this chapter you will learn many interesting spiritual truths about the relationship between the Bible and the joy of the Lord.

The Word of God is filled with the joy of the Lord. God's holy Bible overflows with thousands of supernatural instructions and magnificent promises from your loving Father. The more you get into God's Word, the more the joy of the Lord will flow in you and through you. "...the Word that God speaks is alive and full of power [making it active, operative, energizing, and effective]..." (Hebrews 4:12 AMP)

Please highlight or underline the words "is alive and full of power." The holy Scriptures are spiritually alive. They are filled with the power of God Himself. "...when you received the message of God [which you heard] from us, you welcomed it not as the word of [mere] men, but as it truly is, the Word of God, which is effectually at work in you who believe [exercising its superhuman power in those who adhere to and trust in and rely on it]." (I Thessalonians 2:13 AMP)

You must understand that the holy Bible is very different from books that are written by human beings. Please highlight or underline the words "effectually at work in you who believe" in this verse of

Scripture. The Bible will work effectively in your heart *if* you have faith that it is the absolute truth.

Please highlight or underline the words "exercising its superhuman power in those who adhere to and trust in and rely on it" in the amplification of this verse of Scripture. If you want your heart to sing with joy because the "superhuman power" of God is operating in your life, you must obey God's instructions and have absolute faith in God's promises. "The precepts of the LORD are right, giving joy to the heart..." (Psalm 19:8 NIV)

This verse of Scripture tells you that the Word of God *will* give joy to your heart. If you learn how to continually fill your heart with God's supernatural living Word, your heart will be filled with joy. You will have absolute faith that God's promises are completely reliable. You will consistently react to these magnificent supernatural promises from God instead of reacting negatively to whatever adversity you may face.

You will be like the psalmist who said, "In God, Whose word I praise, in the Lord, Whose word I praise, in God have I put my trust and confident reliance; I will not be afraid. What can man do to me?" (Psalm 56:10-11 AMP)

The psalmist loved God so much that he praised the words that God spoke. The Bible is God's Word to you. Your Father wants you to trust Him and His Word so much that you will not allow anyone or anything to pull you down. You should be like the psalmist who said, "Your testimonies have I taken as a heritage forever, for they are the rejoicing of my heart." (Psalm 119:111 NIV)

Please highlight or underline the words "a heritage forever" in this verse of Scripture. The word "heritage" has the same root as the word "inherit." God's Word has been passed down from your Father to you. God's supernatural Word is eternal – it lasts "forever."

The Word of God will fill your heart if you faithfully obey your Father's instructions to meditate day and night on His Word. Your heart will rejoice if it is filled to overflowing with the supernatural living Word of God.

Think of two or three people who are very close to you. You probably trust these people more than anyone else. If someone you really trusted said that he or she would do something for you, would you believe that this person would do what he or she said? You can believe your Father in heaven *more* than you can believe *any* person here on earth (see Numbers 23:19, Joshua 23:14, I Corinthians 1:9 and Hebrews 6:18).

Know that you can depend totally, completely and absolutely on your Father and on every promise that He has given you in His Word. You should be willing to stake your life on God and His promises if this should be necessary. If you are absolutely certain that God always will do exactly what His Word says He will do, your heart will be filled with joy in the face of adversity.

Your Father has instructed you to renew your mind in His Word each day. He wants you to turn away from the ways of the world. "Do not conform any longer to the pattern of this world, but be transformed by the renewing of your mind...." (Romans 12:2 NIV)

Please highlight or underline the word "transformed" in this verse of Scripture. Your life will be completely changed *if* you faithfully obey your Father's instructions to consistently renew your mind in His Word. "Strip yourselves of your former nature [put off and discard your old unrenewed self] which characterized your previous manner of life and becomes corrupt through lusts and desires that spring from delusion; and be constantly renewed in the spirit of your mind [having a fresh mental and spiritual attitude], and put on the new nature (the regenerate self) created in God's image, [Godlike] in true righteousness and holiness." (Ephesians 4:22-24 AMP)

Please highlight or underline the words *"strip yourselves* of your former nature" in this passage of Scripture. Your Father wants you to faithfully obey His instructions to renew your mind by studying His Word each day so that you will think more and more the way that He thinks instead of thinking the way you used to think.

Please highlight or underline the words "be *constantly* renewed" in this passage of Scripture. The word "constantly" means that your Father wants you to faithfully renew your mind in His Word *each day*. Please highlight or underline the words "having a fresh mental and spiritual attitude" in the amplification of this passage of Scripture. If you constantly renew your mind in God's Word, your attitude will be great. You will become more and more like God.

Your heart will overflow with joy *if* you will study and meditate on God's Word every day of your life. "Do not let this Book of the Law depart from your mouth; meditate on it day and night, so that you may be careful to do everything written in it. Then you will be prosperous and successful." (Joshua 1:8 NIV)

We believe that this verse of Scripture is *vitally important* in these difficult times. Please highlight or underline the words "*Then* you will be prosperous and successful" in the last portion of this verse of Scripture. Your loving Father promises that you *will* be prosperous and successful. There is no asterisk stating that this promise from God is null and void if the economy is not good.

Do you want to be prosperous and successful? Of course you do. Are you consistently doing the three things that your Father has specifically instructed you to do to be prosperous and successful? *Are you* speaking the Word of God continually? *Are you* meditating day and night on the holy Scriptures? *Are you* doing your very best to live your life in complete obedience to the instructions in God's Word?

If you consistently meditate on the Word of God, this constant meditation will create joy within you. We pray that you will obey these three instructions from God so that you will be prosperous and successful as God has promised. "...his delight is in the law of the LORD, and on his law he meditates day and night. He is like a tree planted by streams of water, which yields its fruit in season and whose leaf does not wither. Whatever he does prospers." (Psalm 1:2-3 NIV)

Do you "delight" in the Word of God? When you delight in something, you receive great joy from it. Are you *excited* about meditating day and night on the Word of God? Is consistent Scripture meditation one of the most important priorities in your life?

Please note the correlation once again between meditating "day and night" on the holy Scriptures and prospering in every area of your life. This passage of Scripture says that you will be like a tree that is planted next to a stream of water if you meditate day and night on God's Word.

Visualize an orchard that is planted next to a stream of water. Visualize all of the trees in this orchard being dry and withered and producing no fruit except for the one row of trees that is next to the stream. Visualize these trees being lush and green and loaded with fruit.

Why is this one row of trees so productive when all of the other trees are withered? These trees are able to produce fruit during a drought because their roots are able to reach down to bring water up from the stream when no rain is coming down from the sky.

This picture is what your Father says will happen in *your* life *if* you faithfully obey His instructions to meditate day and night on His Word. Your heart will sing with joy because you will be certain that you will prosper, regardless of the circumstances you face. You will rejoice because you are obeying your Father's specific instructions to meditate day and night on His Word.

The Word of God is one of God's joy-producers. If you renew your mind daily in God's Word and if you obey your Father's instructions to meditate day and night His Word, your heart will be filled with the joy of the Lord.

The Word of God is your spiritual food. If you faithfully obey God's instructions to consistently feed yourself with this supernatural spiritual food that He has provided, you will be like the prophet Jeremiah who said, "When your words came, I ate them; they were my joy and my heart's delight..." (Jeremiah 15:16 KJV)

Are you consistently eating the spiritual food that your Father has provided for you? If you are, God's Word will be your "joy" and your "heart's delight." You will not be able to get enough of the marvelous spiritual food that God has provided. The more you get, the more you will want.

You should feast on this magnificent food that God has given you. You *eat* the spiritual food that God has provided for you by *studying* the holy Scriptures each day. You *digest* this spiritual food by *meditating* day and night on God's Word.

In the world you receive strength and energy from the food that your body is able to *digest*. This same principle applies in the spiritual realm. If you digest your spiritual food by meditating day and night on God's Word, your heart will be filled with supernatural spiritual nourishment. Your heart will sing with joy.

Meditate on God's Word *during* each day and night of your life. If adversity increases, meditate *throughout* the day and night on God's Word. You can eat too much food for good health in your body, but you *cannot* eat too much of the spiritual food that God has provided for you.

Satan and his demons do *not* want your heart to be filled with joy. They want you to have a *heavy heart* that is filled with the negative thoughts they try to put into your mind. Satan and his demons want you to be discouraged.

Your loving Father wants you to be encouraged. Discouragement takes courage *out* of you. Your Father wants you to put supernatural spiritual courage *into* yourself by consistently filling your eyes, your ears, your mind, your heart and your mouth with His Word.

If you faithfully obey your Father's instructions to renew your mind each day and to meditate day and night on His Word, you will consistently make spiritual *deposits* from the holy Bible into your mind and your heart. As this process continues over a period of time, you will have a substantial amount of God's Word on deposit in your heart. Whenever you face difficult problems, you will be able to make spiritual *withdrawals* from God's supernatural living Word that you have deposited into your heart.

You will not allow any adversity you face to steal your joy because you will be able to reach deep down inside of yourself to bring up appropriate promises and instructions from God that apply specifically to whatever challenge you face. "My son, keep my words; lay up within you my commandments [for use when needed] and treasure them." (Proverbs 7:1 AMP)

These words that King Solomon spoke to his son apply to you today. Please highlight or underline the words "lay up within you" in this verse of Scripture. You cannot store up anything that will be more beneficial to you during difficult times than to store up the Word of God in your heart "for use when needed."

The holy Bible is a spiritual *treasure*. Adversity cannot steal your joy if your heart is filled with God's Word. "Great peace have they who love Your law; nothing shall offend them or make them stumble." (Psalm 119:165 AMP)

Do you "love" the Word of God? Do you love God's Word *so much* that you renew your mind in it each day and meditate day and night on it? If you truly love the Word of God, you will consistently experience God's "great peace" in your life. Your heart will be so filled with God's Word that *nothing* will be able to steal God's joy from you.

You will persevere with absolute faith in God regardless of the circumstances you face. "Happy (blessed, fortunate, enviable) is the man who finds skillful and godly Wisdom, and the man who gets understanding [drawing it forth from God's Word and life's experiences], for the gaining of it is better than the gaining of silver, and the profit of it better than fine gold. Skillful and godly Wisdom is more precious than rubies; and nothing you can wish for is to be compared to her." (Proverbs 3:13-15 AMP)

Please highlight or underline the word "happy" at the beginning of this passage of Scripture. You will be happy and filled with the joy of the Lord if you consistently fill your mind and your heart with your Father's supernatural living Word.

As you receive more and more wisdom and understanding from God's Word and from applying the treasure of the holy Bible to your life, you will understand that Scripture meditation is more beneficial than any amount of money you can attain. Nothing in the world can remotely compare to the enormous blessing of a heart that is filled to overflowing with the supernatural living Word of God.

You must not allow any adversity you face to cause you to have a heavy heart. Instead, your heart should be so full of God's Word that it will sing with joy. "Anxiety in a man's heart weighs it down, but an encouraging word makes it glad." (Proverbs 12:25 AMP)

Christians who disobey God's instructions to fill their minds and their hearts each day with His Word will be worried and anxious when they face adversity. They will have a *heavy heart*. Christians who consistently fill their minds and hearts with encouragement from God's

Word will have a *glad heart*, regardless of the circumstances they face.

There *is* a direct relationship between the joy that you experience when you face adversity and the amount of God's Word that fills your mind and your heart. If you faithfully obey your Father's instructions to renew your mind in His Word each day and to meditate day and night on the holy Scriptures and you do this over a period of months and years, your mind and your heart *will* be filled with joy.

Chapter 12

Trust the Lord with All Your Heart

There is a definite relationship between trusting the Lord and not giving up the joy of the Lord. When you face severe adversity, you cannot will yourself not to give up the joy of the Lord. You should trust the Lord *so deeply* that you are absolutely certain that He *will* fulfill His promises and bring you safely through whatever problems you face.

One of the primary reasons why some Christians do not manifest the joy of the Lord is that they do not trust Him completely to bring them safely through whatever problems they face. Some Christians give up their joy because they either are ignorant of God's promises or they do not have absolute faith that God *will* do exactly what He says He will do.

There is a definite relationship between being filled with the joy of the Lord and consistently filling your mind and your heart with God's Word. You have seen that your Father has specifically instructed you to renew your mind in His Word every day. He has instructed you to meditate day and night on the holy Scriptures.

If you faithfully obey these instructions from God, your faith in God *will* increase steadily. You will react with joy regardless of the circumstances you face because you will trust God completely. If you are not consistent in renewing your mind each day and meditating day and night on God's Word, you will give Satan's demons and any adversity you face an opportunity to steal the joy of the Lord from you.

When you face seemingly severe problems, you must not focus on those problems. You must know specific promises from God's Word that apply to whatever problems you face. Focus continually on these promises from God.

Thank your Father for these magnificent promises that He has given to you. Praise Him. Worship Him. Rejoice continually. "…No man who believes in Him [who adheres to, relies on, and trusts in Him] will [ever] be put to shame or be disappointed." (Romans 10:11 AMP)

Please highlight or underline the words "no man" in this verse of Scripture. These words include *you*. If you have absolute faith in God, you will *never* be disappointed. Your Father will honor your faith in Him if you know what His Word says and if you absolutely refuse to give up, persevering in your faith in Him. "God is faithful (reliable, trustworthy, and therefore ever true to His promise, and He can be depended on)…" (I Corinthians 1:9 AMP)

Please highlight or underline the words "God is faithful (reliable, trustworthy, and therefore ever true to His promise" in this verse of Scripture and the amplification. God is completely dependable.

If you know that God is in complete control, regardless of what the circumstances look like, you will not give up your joy. You will refuse to allow the problems you face to pull you down because you will be certain that Jesus Christ already has carried the heavy load of these problems for you. "Surely He has borne our griefs (sicknesses, weaknesses, and distresses) and carried our sorrows…" (Isaiah 53:4 AMP)

These prophetic words from Isaiah refer to Jesus Christ. Please highlight or underline the word "surely" in this verse of Scripture. There is no doubt whatsoever that Jesus *already* has carried the heavy load of whatever problems you face. You do *not* have to carry this load again.

Thank Jesus for carrying the burdens you face. Praise Him and rejoice continually because you are absolutely certain that He has carried the heavy burdens for you. Jesus said, "Come unto me, all ye that labour and are heavy laden, and I will give you rest." (Matthew 11:28 KJV)

Please highlight or underline the words "Come unto me, all ye that labour and are heavy laden" in this verse of Scripture. The word "all" includes you. Refuse to struggle and strain. Give the heavy burdens to Jesus and *leave* them with Him. If you do, He *"will* give you rest." "...he who has once entered [God's] rest also has ceased from [the weariness and pain] of human labors..." (Hebrews 4:10 AMP)

Please highlight or underline the words "ceased from [the weariness and pain] of human labors" in this verse of Scripture and the amplification. If you struggle and strain, you are denying the finished work of Jesus Christ. Relax. Trust Jesus completely.

If you faithfully obey Jesus' instructions to give every problem to Him, you will be filled with His joy regardless of the circumstances you face. "Casting the whole of your care [all your anxieties, all your worries, all your concerns, once and for all] on Him, for He cares for you affectionately and cares about you watchfully." (I Peter 5:7 AMP)

Please highlight or underline the words "the whole," the three times the word "all" is used and the words "once and for all" in this verse of Scripture and the amplification. Your Father instructs you to give *every* problem to Him. He wants you to know that He cares about what you are going through and that He is watching over you. "Cast your burden on the Lord [releasing the weight of it] and He will sustain you; He will never allow the [consistently] righteous to be moved (made to slip, fall, or fail). " (Psalm 55:22 AMP)

Please highlight or underline the words "Cast your burden on the Lord [releasing the weight of it]" in this verse of Scripture and the amplification. If you are fishing and you *cast* your line into the water, you actually throw this weighted line into the water. *Throw* your problems to the Lord. Let go of them. Give Him the problems you face. Leave them with Him.

Why should you let go of the problems you face? You should give the problems to the Lord because you are absolutely certain that "He *will* sustain you." The word "sustain" means to provide support. God will support you.

He will do His part. You must do your part. God's part is to sustain you. Your part is to give your burdens to Him and leave them with Him. "…whoever leans on, trusts in, and is confident in the Lord – happy, blessed, and fortunate is he." (Proverbs 16:20 AMP)

The word "whoever" in this verse of Scripture includes *you*. You will be "happy, blessed, and fortunate" *if* you "lean on, trust in, and are confident in the Lord." There is no question that there is a definite relationship between experiencing the joy of the Lord and trusting completely in Him. "Our inner selves wait [earnestly] for the Lord; He is our Help and our Shield. For in Him does our heart rejoice, because we have trusted (relied on and been confident) in His holy name." (Psalm 33:20-21 AMP)

Please highlight or underline the words "inner selves" in this passage of Scripture. Your inner self is what you are deep down inside of yourself. The Bible refers to your inner self as the hidden person of your heart. (see I Peter 3:4).

Rejoice deep down inside of yourself, regardless of the circumstances you face. If you truly believe that the Lord will help you and protect you, you will rejoice because of your absolute confidence in Him.

Your Father does not want you to react to the circumstances you face. He wants you to react with absolute faith in His Word. He wants you to speak "…of the nonexistent things that [He has foretold and promised] as if they [already] existed." (Romans 4:17 AMP)

Your heart should be so filled with faith in God that you will speak of the promises He has given to you "as if they [already] existed." Your Father wants your faith in Him to be like the faith of Abraham.

When Abraham was almost one hundred years old and God told him that his elderly wife would give birth to a child, Abraham absolutely believed what God said, …He did not weaken in faith when he considered the [utter] impotence of his own body, which was as good as dead because he was about a hundred years old, or [when he considered] the barrenness of Sarah's [deadened] womb. No unbelief or distrust made him waver (doubtingly question) concerning the promise of God, but he grew strong and was empowered by faith as he gave praise and glory to God, fully satisfied and assured that God was able and mighty to keep His word and to do what He had promised." (Romans 4:19-21 AMP)

Please highlight or underline the words "he gave praise and glory to God" in this passage of Scripture. Praise God and thank Him even if you face what seems to be an impossible situation. Have absolute faith that your Father will do exactly what His Word says He will do.

You should trust the Lord completely whenever you are going through a season of adversity. "To every thing there is a season, and a time to every purpose under the heaven" (Ecclesiastes 3:1 KJV)

Please highlight or underline the words "every thing" in this verse of Scripture. These words include whatever problems *you* face at this time. A season has a beginning and an end. This season of adversity will not last indefinitely. Trust the Lord's timing just as you trust Him in every other area. You should be like the psalmist who said, "...I will hope continually, and will praise You yet more and more." (Psalm 71:14 AMP)

Please highlight or underline the words "I will hope continually" in this verse of Scripture. The psalmist refused to give up hope. He praised the Lord again and again in the face of seemingly severe problems.

Your Father wants you to do the same thing. "Let us then fearlessly and confidently and boldly draw near to the throne of grace (the throne of God's unmerited favor to us sinners), that we may receive mercy [for our failures] and find grace to help in good time for every need [appropriate help and well-timed help, coming just when we need it]." (Hebrews 4:16 AMP)

Please highlight or underline the words "fearlessly and confidently and boldly" in this verse of Scripture. These words explain exactly how your Father wants you to come to Him in prayer. God does not expect you to be perfect. Trust Him to have "mercy for your failures."

Please highlight or underline the words "find grace to help in good time for every need" in this verse of Scripture. Why would you ever give up your joy if you are absolutely certain that God will help you with *every* need just as He says He will?

Please highlight or underline the words "appropriate help and well-timed help, coming just when we need it" in the amplification of this verse of Scripture. Know that your Father will help you in His way and in His perfect timing.

Do not give up your joy. Keep trusting God to give you exactly what you need just when you need it. "…be invigorated and strengthened with all power according to the might of His glory, [to exercise] every kind of endurance and patience (perseverance and forbearance) with joy" (Colossians 1:11 AMP)

Please highlight or underline the words "be invigorated and strengthened with *all* power" in this verse of Scripture. God would not have told you that you could receive *all* power if He will not do exactly what He says He will do. Receive by faith the supernatural power of Almighty God in your life.

Please highlight or underline the words "every kind of endurance and patience (perseverance and forbearance) *with joy*" in this verse of Scripture and the amplification. Refuse to give up. Rejoice. Keep on rejoicing. Know that your Father is with you whenever you face adversity.

One of the most important things you can do to maintain the joy of the Lord in your life is to consistently increase your faith in God. Our book titled *Unshakable Faith in Almighty God* is filled with hundreds of facts from God's Word telling you exactly what your Father instructs you to do to increase your faith in Him. Our Scripture Meditation Cards and the accompanying CD that are titled *Continually Increasing Faith in God* are filled with facts from the Bible that will help you to increase your faith in God.

If you will learn and obey the specific scriptural instructions your Father has given you to increase your faith in Him, your joy will be full. You will have so much faith in God that you will persevere in faith, regardless of the seeming severity of the problems you face.

Chapter 13

Focus Continually on the Lord

You have learned that strong faith in God requires a close and intimate relationship with God. You have seen the importance of continually filling your eyes, your ears, your mind, your heart and your mouth with God's supernatural living Word. In this chapter you will see several additional verses of Scripture that instruct you to focus continually on the Lord, regardless of the circumstances you face.

When God created you, He gave you the ability to choose. You use this ability throughout every day of your life. When you face difficult circumstances, you must make the choice between focusing on adversity or focusing on God. "You will guard him and keep him in perfect and constant peace whose mind [both its inclination and its character] is stayed on You, because he commits himself to You, leans on You, and hopes confidently in You." (Isaiah 26:3 AMP)

Please highlight or underline the words "You will guard him and keep him in perfect and constant peace" in this verse of Scripture. The word "You" refers to God. Do you want Almighty God to "guard" you and to keep you "in perfect and constant peace?" Of course you do. God has said *what He will do*. However, you must do *your* part.

Please highlight or underline the words "stayed on You" in this verse of Scripture. You *will* experience perfect and constant peace if you *keep* your mind focused on God, absolutely refusing to focus on whatever challenges you face.

Why should you keep your mind focused on God? Please highlight or underline the words "because he commits himself to You, leans on You, and hopes confidently in You" in this verse of Scripture. Your mind *will* be filled with God's supernatural peace *if* you are totally committed to God, if you lean on Him and if all of your hope and confidence is in Him.

You should be like the psalmist who said, "I have set the Lord continually before me; because He is at my right hand, I shall not be moved. Therefore my heart is glad and my glory [my inner self] rejoices…" (Psalm 16:8-9 AMP)

Please highlight or underline the words "continually before me" in this passage of Scripture. The psalmist did what Isaiah 26:3 instructs each of us to do. He focused *continually* on the Lord.

Please highlight or underline the words "I shall not be moved." The psalmist was *not* affected by the problems he faced. Therefore, his heart was "glad." He consistently *rejoiced* deep within himself.

We live in difficult times. At the time this book is being written, the news media frequently pours out bad news. You must understand the absolute importance of focusing continually on the Lord instead of allowing yourself to focus on the constant barrage of bad news from the world. "…we walk by faith [we regulate our lives and conduct ourselves by our conviction or belief respecting man's relationship to God and divine things, with trust and holy fervor; thus we walk] not by sight or appearance." (II Corinthians 5:7 AMP)

Please highlight or underline the words "we walk by faith" in this verse of Scripture. These four words are vitally important. Your Father wants you to walk *by faith* throughout every hour of every day of your life.

Please highlight or underline the words "not by sight or appearance" in this verse of Scripture. Your life should *not* be controlled by external circumstances. Your life should be dominated by your absolute faith in God. You should focus on God at all times because you trust Him completely.

If you focus on the problems you face, you give Satan and his demons an opportunity to influence your thinking. You do exactly what Satan's demons want you to do. You give them an opportunity to hammer away at your mind with negative thoughts concerning the problems you face.

Develop the habit of immediately going to God whenever you face adversity. You must learn from the holy Bible how to remain filled with God's power and glory instead of reacting to bad news.

This book is filled with Scripture that tells you what God says about reacting to adversity. Pray the Bible back to God, using Scripture verses that apply to whatever problem you face. If you pray with unwavering faith in God and the reliability of His Word, you will not be defeated emotionally by the problems you face.

Instead of focusing on problems and giving an opportunity to Satan and his demons, you should focus continually on Jesus Christ. "Let us fix our eyes on Jesus, the author and perfecter of our faith, who for the joy set before him endured the cross, scorning its shame, and sat down at the right hand of the throne of God. Consider him who endured such opposition from sinful men, so that you will not grow weary and lose heart." (Hebrews 12:2-3 NIV)

Please highlight or underline the words "fix our eyes on Jesus" in this passage of Scripture. If you focus continually on Jesus Who is the "author and perfecter" of your faith, your faith in Him will be deep, strong and unwavering.

You will follow the example of Jesus Who refused to give up His joy. Jesus "endured the cross" because of "the joy set before Him." He saw through the agony of His crucifixion to the eternal joy of the multitudes of people who would live eternally with Him in the glory of heaven because they trusted Him completely for their eternal salvation.

When you face seemingly severe problems, consider what Jesus did when He was crucified by "sinful men." Do "not grow weary and lose heart." Fix your eyes on Jesus. Refuse to give up your joy. See past the temporary ordeal that you face.

In Chapter 7 you read many facts from the Bible pertaining to the victory that Jesus won for you. In Chapter 10 you saw additional facts from the Bible that show you that Jesus lives in your heart. If

Jesus is your Savior, the joy in your life will be constant if you focus continually on the victorious Jesus Christ Who lives in *your* heart.

Jesus already has won a total, complete and absolute victory over every problem you will ever face. Will you focus continually on the victorious Jesus Christ Who lives in your heart or will you give in to your emotions and the influence of Satan and his demons and focus on the problems you face?

You see a good example of focusing on the Lord when Moses approached the Red Sea. "...he never flinched but held staunchly to his purpose and endured steadfastly as one who gazed on Him Who is invisible." (Hebrews 11:27 AMP)

This verse of Scripture describes the magnificent focus of Moses as he approached the Red Sea with a powerful Egyptian army behind him, high mountains to his right and left and the large and deep Red Sea ahead of him.

Please highlight or underline the words "he never flinched but held staunchly to his purpose and endured steadfastly" in this verse of Scripture. Moses refused to be deterred by the seemingly impossible circumstances he faced. He persevered and kept moving forward.

Please highlight or underline the words "as one who gazed on Him Who is invisible" in this verse of Scripture. Even though Moses could not see the Lord with his natural eyesight, he still focused continually on Him.

God honored this magnificent focus of Moses. God parted the waves of the Red Sea so that Moses and the Israelites could pass safely through on dry ground. When Pharaoh and his army came, the water returned to destroy them (see the fourteenth chapter of Exodus.) *Know* that God will honor your faith if you focus on Him continually and refuse to allow whatever problems you face to overwhelm you.

You will see a similar example of unwavering focus from a man of God if you read what King Jehoshaphat did when he faced a mighty army that was far superior to his army. King Jehoshaphat said, "...we have no power to face this vast army that is attacking us. We do not know what to do, but our eyes are upon you." (II Chronicles 20:12 NIV)

Please highlight or underline the words "we have no power" and the words "we do not know what to do" in this verse of Scripture. King Jehoshaphat openly admitted that his army did not have the power they needed and that he did not know what to do.

What did King Jehoshaphat do? He focused continually on the Lord. He refused to focus on the tremendous superiority of the opposing army. He did what you should do when you face seemingly severe adversity – he focused continually on God.

If you follow God's instructions to focus continually on Him, your Father *will* bless you when you face difficult problems. The Bible speaks of "…God, Who comforts and encourages and refreshes and cheers the depressed and the sinking…" (II Corinthians 7:6 AMP)

Do you feel depressed because of the problems you face? Do you feel like you are sinking? Focus continually on God if the problems in your life seem to be too much for you. Know that He will do exactly what He says He will do when He says that He *will* "comfort and encourage and refresh and cheer" you. Receive these blessings by faith.

Your Father does *not* want you to worry about the future (see Matthew 6:34). He wants you to live one day at a time, trusting Him completely to bring you through that day.

Refuse to allow anxiety to get into your heart. Meditate day and night on the supernatural living Word of God so that you will consistently fill your heart with encouragement from the holy Scriptures. You *will* have a glad heart if you faithfully obey God's instructions in this area.

If you continually rejoice because your heart is filled with joy, you will laugh a lot, regardless of the circumstances you face. The next chapter is filled with facts pertaining to laughter. You will be blessed if you laugh a lot because you have absolute faith in the Lord.

Chapter 14

Laugh Because Your Heart Is Filled with Joy

You have just seen several verses of Scripture that instruct you to focus continually on the Lord instead of focusing on the problems you face. If you refuse to focus on circumstances, you will be able to laugh in the face of adversity.

People in the world laugh when they are happy. They laugh when circumstances are favorable and everything is going well. That is automatic, but God's ways are very different from the ways of the world.

When you face seemingly unsolvable problems, you should praise the Lord and thank Him. You should rejoice. You should laugh. You should act the same way you would act if these problems *already* had been solved.

Abraham Lincoln was a devout Christian. President Lincoln led the United States throughout the Civil War. He often told jokes at Cabinet meetings to break the tension caused by the severe problems the members of the Cabinet were discussing. President Lincoln once said, "With the fearful strain that is on me night and day, if I did not laugh I should die."

Winston Churchill was the prime minister of Great Britain during World War II. Mr. Churchill was a hero to the British people because he persevered in the face of many severe problems. He once said, "We cannot deal with the most serious things in the world unless we understand the amusing." Winston Churchill often demonstrated a unique sense of humor during the adversity he faced. Like Abraham

Lincoln, he understood the relationship between a sense of humor and coping with adversity.

If you faithfully obey your Father's instructions to rejoice, to praise Him, to thank Him and to laugh when you face adversity, your faith in God will increase. The laughter that comes out of your mouth at a time when laughter seems to be completely illogical is clear evidence that you are trusting God. "He will yet fill your mouth with laughter and your lips with shouts of joy." (Job 8:21 NIV)

God created human beings with an ability to laugh that He did not give to any other species that He created. Please highlight or underline the words "He will yet fill your mouth with laughter" in this verse of Scripture. God obviously wants you to laugh because *He* fills your mouth with laughter.

Please highlight or underline the words "your lips with shouts of joy." In a subsequent chapter we will study several verses of Scripture that instruct you to shout for joy. Your Father wants your heart to be so filled with joy that the abundance of joy will pour out of your mouth.

Why would anyone actually laugh and shout with joy in the face of adversity? If you have faithfully obeyed your Father's specific instructions to meditate day and night on His Word, your heart will be filled with many promises and instructions from God.

The power of God's Word in your heart will be much greater than any problems you face. You will be able to laugh in the face of adversity because your heart is overflowing with the enormous supernatural power of the Word of God.

If you are certain that every promise in the Bible is absolutely true, completely reliable and totally dependable, you will not allow the problems you face to pull you down. Instead, the joy of the Lord will flow out of your mouth when you face adversity. You *will* laugh in the face of adversity *if* you know what God promises to do and *if* you are absolutely certain that your Father will do what He promises.

You must not allow negative emotions to control you when you face adversity. If you genuinely laugh at these problems, you will direct your emotions instead of allowing your emotions to control you.

When God created you He gave you emotions to be your servant, not your master. You must not allow your emotions to control you. Some people are extremely emotional. They go through a lot of emotional ups and downs.

Your Father does not want you to allow yourself to become emotionally low. He will test your emotions to show you where you stand emotionally. He wants your heart to be so programmed with His Word that you will laugh spontaneously when you face adversity.

God has provided everything you need to keep your emotions under control. He has given you the holy Bible so that you can program yourself with His Word. He has assured you that He makes His home in your heart and that He is with you at all times.

Andrew Carnegie was a very successful businessman and philanthropist in the last part of the nineteenth century and the early years of the twentieth century. Mr. Carnegie once said, "My young partners do the work and I do the laughing. I recommend to you that there is little success where there is little laughing."

Satan and his demons do *not* want you to laugh when you face adversity. They do their best to put thoughts of worry, doubt, fear and anxiety in your mind. They want you to be discouraged and frustrated. When you respond to adversity with laughter, Satan and his demons are frustrated and irritated.

Mark Twain was a nineteenth century humorist and journalist. Mr. Twain faced a great deal of adversity in his life, but he seldom lost his sense of humor. He once said, "The human race has only one effective weapon and that is laughter."

You must not take yourself too seriously. One of the most important lessons that some of us need to learn is to *laugh at ourselves*. God wants you to take Him seriously. He wants you to take His Word seriously. He wants you to laugh at yourself.

Laughter is God's shock absorber. There is a definite relationship between your health and a heart that is filled with joy and laughter. "A happy heart is good medicine and a cheerful mind works healing..." (Proverbs 17:22 AMP)

Please highlight or underline the words "good medicine" in this verse of Scripture. Your Father has provided supernatural spiritual medicine for you. You will partake of this spiritual medicine if you consistently fill your mind and your heart with His Word by faithfully obeying His instructions to study His Word each day and to meditate day and night on the holy Scriptures.

Please highlight or underline the words "works healing" in this verse of Scripture. If you obey your Father's instructions to renew your mind in His Word each day, you will have "a cheerful mind." You must understand the relationship between a cheerful mind, a happy heart, laughing in the face of adversity, enjoying good health and receiving healing when you are sick.

If you allow the problems you face to discourage you, this negative reaction to adversity often will cause you to become sick. If your mind and your heart are filled with joy and you laugh at adversity, this joy will help you to be healed.

In 1964 a man named Norman Cousins faced a seemingly severe illness. His doctors informed him that the connective tissue in his spine was deteriorating and that he did not have long to live.

Norman Cousins refused to dwell on this diagnosis. He obtained a movie projector and many humorous films, including several Marx Brothers movies. He watched these movies one after another. He laughed so hard at the movies that his health improved. His book titled *Anatomy of an Illness* explained how he laughed his way back to health.

If this man was able to laugh his way back to health because he watched funny movies, think of the relationship that exists between the joy of the Lord and good health in your life.

Researchers at the University of Maryland School of Medicine in Baltimore did a study on the relationship between laughter and good health. The results of this study were presented to the American Heart Association meeting in New Orleans in 2008.

This and similar studies have shown that happy people recover from sickness more rapidly than sad people. Laughter reduces the level of stress hormones in the body. Laughter increases the level of health-enhancing hormones such as endorphins.

Medical science has proven on many occasions that a great deal of sickness is caused by worry, anxiety, fear and other negative reactions to adversity. This book is filled with *facts* pertaining to the joy of the Lord. If you consistently study and meditate on the Scripture in this book and obey your Father's instructions, you *will* laugh in the face of adversity. Your health will be much better than it would be if you allow the problems you face to pull you down.

Chapter 15

Rejoice in the Lord at All Times

The key word that we will discuss in this chapter is the word "rejoice." The Greek word "chiro" that is translated as "rejoice" in the following verse of Scripture and on the cover of this book means "to be cheerful, calmly happy or well off." *Webster's New World Dictionary* says that to rejoice is "to be glad, happy or delighted – full of joy." "Rejoice in the Lord always [delight, gladden yourselves in Him]; again I say, Rejoice!" (Philippians 4:4 AMP)

Please highlight or underline the word "always" in this verse of Scripture. Your Father has instructed you to rejoice at *all* times, *regardless* of what is happening to you. This instruction does not make sense from a logical and intellectual worldly perspective. "'For my thoughts are not your thoughts, neither are your ways my ways,' declares the LORD. As the heavens are higher than the earth, so are my ways higher than your ways and my thoughts than your thoughts.'" (Isaiah 55:8-9 NIV)

From a worldly perspective, severe problems and rejoicing do not go together. You have just seen that you are instructed to rejoice in the Lord continually. God often uses repetition for purposes of emphasis. When He begins and ends one short verse of Scripture with the same word "rejoice" and He adds the word "always" to this instruction, you can be certain that your Father is emphasizing that He wants *you* to rejoice in Him at all times.

Please highlight or underline the words "delight, gladden your-selves in Him" in the amplification of Philippians 4:4. *If* every area of your life revolves around the Lord and *if* you have absolute faith in Him, your heart *will* sing with joy regardless of the circumstances you face.

Your Father does not want you to go through emotional ups and downs. He does not want you to have good days and bad days. God instructs you to rejoice in Him at all times because He is *much* greater and much more powerful than *any* problem you will ever face.

You should rejoice in the Lord whether you feel like rejoicing or not. Every aspect of your life should be dictated by the Word of God and the Spirit of God filling your heart. Shortly after the instructions you have just read in Philippians 4:4, the apostle Paul said, "...I have learned how to be content (satisfied to the point where I am not dis-turbed or disquieted) in whatever state I am." (Philippians 4:11 AMP)

Please highlight or underline the words "*not* disturbed or disqui-eted in *whatever* state I am" in this verse of Scripture and the ampli-fication. Paul said that he *learned* how to be calm, quiet and confi-dent at all times regardless of the circumstances he faced. If the apostle Paul learned how to react in this way, *you* can learn this same lesson.

You decide how you will react to adversity. You should be deter-mined to *always* rejoice in the Lord and to remain quiet, calm and confident in the face of *all* adversity. You should do what Jesus in-structed you to do when He said, "Do not let your hearts be troubled (distressed, agitated). You believe in and adhere to and trust in and rely on God..." (John 14:1 AMP)

Please highlight or underline the words "Do not let your hearts be troubled (distressed, agitated)" in this verse of Scripture and the am-plification. The word "let" is very important. Your heart can only be troubled, distressed and agitated with your permission.

You must not allow your emotions to control you, regardless of the seeming severity of the problems you face. *How* can you achieve this goal? You will determine your emotional reaction if you obey God's instructions to constantly immerse yourself in His Word.

You are instructed to *believe* in God. You should have absolute faith that God Who lives in your heart is much greater and much more powerful than any problem you face. Trust Him completely.

Jesus told you to *adhere* to God – to learn His instructions and to faithfully obey them. This book is filled with facts from God's holy Word telling you *how* to rejoice in the face of adversity and *how* to remain calm, quiet and confident because you trust God completely. "Blessed (happy, fortunate, to be envied) is the man whom You discipline and instruct, O Lord, and teach out of Your law, that You may give him power to keep himself calm in the days of adversity..." (Psalm 94:12-13 AMP)

Please highlight or underline the words "You discipline and instruct, O Lord, and teach out of Your law" in this passage of Scripture. Study and meditate day and night on the scriptural instructions in this book that tell you how to rejoice at all times and how to remain calm, quiet and confident in the face of adversity. *Do* exactly what your Father instructs you to do. Jesus said, "...Do not be seized with alarm and struck with fear; only keep on believing." (Mark 5:36 AMP)

Stay calm. Rejoice. Praise God. Thank Him. *Keep on believing.* Make up your mind that you *will* rejoice at *all* times as your Father has instructed you to do. Turn away from logical and intellectual worldly thinking to do what the holy Bible instructs you to do. "Be happy [in your faith] and rejoice and be glad-hearted continually (always)" (I Thessalonians 5:16 AMP)

Please highlight or underline the words "Be happy [in your faith]" in this verse of Scripture and the amplification. Your faith in God is the key to continually experiencing the joy of the Lord in your life. You *will* have a glad heart if your faith in God is deep, strong and unwavering.

Please highlight or underline the words "continually (always)" in this verse of Scripture and the amplification. Once again your Father instructs you to rejoice *at all times* regardless of the circumstances you face.

You are instructed to rejoice in the Lord continually because of your absolute certainty that He has given you victory over every problem you face (see Deuteronomy 28:13, John 16:33, Romans 8:37, II

Corinthians 2:14 and I John 5:4-5). If you have absolute faith that your Father will do exactly what He says He will do, you *will* rejoice while you are faithfully waiting for Him to fulfill His promises (see Romans 12:12, Galatians 6:9 and Hebrews 3:6).

Your Father lives in your heart. He is with you at all times. Focus on God and His indwelling presence instead of focusing on the problems you face (see Zephaniah 3:17, I Corinthians 3:16, II Corinthians 13:5, Ephesians 3:17 and Colossians 2:10). Your Father promises to meet *all* of your needs (see Psalm 34:10, Romans 8:32, Philippians 4:19 and II Peter 1:3).

The holy Bible instructs you to rejoice continually, regardless of the circumstances you face. Your Father does not want you to give up hope. He wants you to rejoice with patience and perseverance. "Rejoice and exult in hope; be steadfast and patient in suffering and tribulation; be constant in prayer." (Romans 12:12 AMP)

The apostle Paul was imprisoned on several occasions because of his faith in Jesus Christ. Paul often was beaten. He was close to death many times. Paul said that he was faced "…with far more imprisonments, [beaten] with countless stripes, and frequently [at the point of] death. Five times I received from [the hands of] the Jews forty [lashes all] but one; three times I have been beaten with rods; once I was stoned. Three times I have been aboard a ship wrecked at sea; a [whole] night and a day I have spent [adrift] on the deep" (II Corinthians 11:23-25 AMP)

This man who instructed you to rejoice at *all* times obviously was not giving you theoretical advice. Paul also said, "Many times on journeys, [exposed to] perils from rivers, perils from bandits, perils from [my own] nation, perils from the Gentiles, perils in the city, perils in the desert places, perils in the sea, perils from those posing as believers [but destitute of Christian knowledge and piety]; in toil and hardship, watching often [through sleepless nights], in hunger and thirst, frequently driven to fasting by want, in cold and exposure and lack of clothing." (II Corinthians 11:26-27 AMP)

Paul did not enjoy an easy life. You must understand the context from which he wrote his anointed instructions telling you to rejoice at all times. If Paul could learn to be quiet and content regardless of the severe adversity he faced, *you* can learn to react in this way too.

This chapter is filled with specific instructions from your Father telling you to rejoice at all times regardless of the circumstances you face. These instructions are the key to everything else we will explain from the holy Scriptures regarding the joy of the Lord. *Refuse* to allow the circumstances you face to steal your joy.

Chapter 16

Joy in the Face of Adversity

The apostle Paul did not allow the many trials and tribulations that he faced to discourage him. Instead, his heart was filled with joy when he faced adversity. Paul said, "...I am greatly encouraged; in all our troubles my joy knows no bounds." (II Corinthians 7:4 NIV)

Please highlight or underline the words "in all our troubles." Paul said that he was "greatly encouraged" *whenever* he faced trouble. He said that his joy was *unlimited*.

This reaction is very different from the way that unbelievers and some Christians react to adversity. Paul's reaction is consistent with the scriptural instructions that you read in Chapter 15. *Why wouldn't you* react with great joy if you are *absolutely certain* that God *is* with you whenever you face adversity and if you *know* that He will help you as He says He will (see Psalm 121:21, Isaiah 41:13, Hebrews 2:18, 4:16 and 13:6)?

If you turn to the Lord with absolute and unwavering faith when you are in trouble, you can be certain that He will honor your faith in Him. He will bring you safely through the problems you face in His way and in His good timing. "When the righteous cry for help, the Lord hears, and delivers them out of all their distress and troubles." (Psalm 34:17 AMP)

Please highlight or underline the words "delivers them out of *all* their distress and troubles" in this verse of Scripture. This word "all" includes whatever problem *you* face at this time.

If you are tempted to give up your joy, meditate repeatedly on this verse of Scripture. Speak this great truth from God again and again. *Know* that your Father will deliver you out of every problem you face if you will persevere with deep, strong and unwavering faith in Him.

You may go through a season of adversity, but you can trust God completely. Persevere in your faith in God. "…weeping may endure for a night, but joy cometh in the morning." (Psalm 30:5 KJV)

Please highlight or underline the words "joy cometh in the morning" in this verse of Scripture. Refuse to allow adversity to steal your joy.

God never said that you will not face adversity, but He has repeatedly promised to bring you *through* whatever adversity you face if you have unwavering faith in Him. "Those who sow in tears will reap with songs of joy." (Psalm 126:5 NIV)

Please highlight or underline the words "*will* reap with songs of joy" in this verse of Scripture. Before a farmer can *reap* a harvest, he first must *sow* seeds. This same principle of sowing and reaping applies in your life whenever you face adversity (see Galatians 6:7-9).

The Bible is a spiritual seed (see Luke 8:11). Consistently plant the seeds of God's supernatural living Word into your eyes, your ears, your mind, your heart and your mouth. If you consistently sow the seeds of God's Word when you face adversity, you will reap a harvest of joy when you come safely out on the other side. Jesus said, "…your sorrow shall be turned into joy." (John 16:20 KJV)

The Bible is filled with hundreds of specific instructions telling you exactly what you should do when you face adversity. Often what seems to be the worst thing that could happen to you will turn out to be a blessing if you react to the adversity you face according to God's instructions and promises in His Word, the Bible.

You should always take a long term view when you face adversity. *Rejoice* in the face of adversity because you know that your Father *will* cause you to grow and mature if you react to adversity according to His specific instructions. "…we rejoice in the hope of the glory of God. Not only so, but we also rejoice in our sufferings, because we know that suffering produces perseverance; perseverance, character; and character, hope." (Romans 5:2-4 NIV)

Please highlight or underline the words "we also rejoice in our suffering" in this passage of Scripture. *Why* does the Bible instruct you to rejoice when you suffer? Please highlight or underline the words "perseverance," "character" and "hope" in this verse of Scripture. If you react to adversity the way that God's Word instructs you to react, your perseverance will increase, your character will improve and you will have hope for the future.

Faithfully obey your Father's instructions to rejoice whenever you face adversity. "Beloved, do not be amazed and bewildered at the fiery ordeal which is taking place to test your quality, as though something strange (unusual and alien to you and your position) were befalling you. But insofar as you are sharing Christ's sufferings, rejoice, so that when His glory [full of radiance and splendor] is revealed, you may also rejoice with triumph [exultantly]." (I Peter 4:12-13 AMP)

This passage of Scripture says that "you are sharing Christ's sufferings" when you face severe problems. Right after these words, you are instructed to *rejoice* because you are certain that you will come safely through this adversity. As you trust God, He will make you into a person that you never dreamed you could become.

You should rejoice when you face adversity because you are certain that this reaction will result in tremendous blessings in your life. "…after you have suffered a little while, the God of all grace [Who imparts all blessing and favor], Who has called you to His [own] eternal glory in Christ Jesus, will Himself complete and make you what you ought to be, establish and ground you securely, and strengthen, and settle you." (I Peter 5:10 AMP)

Please highlight or underline the words "after you have suffered *a little while*" in this verse of Scripture. Trust your Father not to allow you to suffer beyond your capacity to endure. You can have absolute faith that your Father "*will* Himself complete and make you what you ought to be, establish and ground you securely, and strengthen, and settle you."

Always do your best to look at whatever adversity you face from God's perspective instead of the limited perspective of the intellectual and logical reasoning of the world. Rejoice when you face adversity because you know that your Father will use your faith in Him to cause you to grow and mature to become what He wants you to become.

We repeatedly emphasize that God's ways are *very different* from the ways of the world (see Isaiah 55:8-9). When you face adversity, you should rejoice *because your Father has instructed you to rejoice.* "Consider it pure joy, my brothers, whenever you face trials of many kinds, because you know that the testing of your faith develops perseverance. Perseverance must finish its work so that you may be mature and complete, not lacking anything." (James 1:2-4 NIV)

Please highlight or underline the words "pure joy" in this passage of Scripture. These words are included to tell you exactly how you are instructed to react "whenever you face trials." *Do* what your Father has instructed you to do.

Rejoice because you know that reacting to adversity with absolute faith in God will increase your perseverance. You will "be mature and complete, not lacking anything" if you react with unwavering faith in God and if you rejoice when you face adversity. "…by sorrow of heart the spirit is broken." (Proverbs 15:13 AMP)

Please highlight or underline the words "sorrow of heart" in this verse of Scripture. Your heart should be so full of God's Word that sorrow cannot enter into it and remain there. You do not want your spirit to be broken. This will not happen to you if your heart is filled to overflowing with God's Word (see Psalm 37:31, Proverbs 4:20-23 and Colossians 3:16).

Your faith in God should be so strong that you will continually share your faith with others. If you do, you *can* expect to be persecuted sooner or later. The apostle Paul often experienced persecution. "…the Jews stirred up the devout women of high rank and the outstanding men of the town, and instigated persecution against Paul and Barnabas and drove them out of their boundaries." (Acts 13:50 AMP)

Paul and Barnabas were persecuted by the Jews and driven out of town. *How* did Paul and Barnabas react? They reacted to this persecution exactly the way that the Lord has instructed *you* to react whenever you are persecuted because of your faith in Christ. "…[the apostles] shook off the dust from their feet against them and went to Iconium. And the disciples were continually filled [throughout their souls] with joy and the Holy Spirit." (Acts 13:51-52 AMP)

Please highlight or underline the words "shook off the dust from their feet against them and went to Iconium" in this passage of Scripture. Refuse to identify with any persecution you receive because of your faith in Christ. Move on. Do whatever the Lord calls you to do next.

Please highlight or underline the words "continually filled [throughout their souls] with joy and the Holy Spirit" in this passage of Scripture and the amplification. Your heart will sing with joy that is produced by the Holy Spirit if you refuse to allow persecution to stop you from sharing Christ with unbelievers.

Paul and Barnabas knew that they were doing what God called them to do. They went on to the next town, absolutely refusing to give up the joy of the Lord. Your Father wants you to do the same whenever you are persecuted because of your faith in Christ.

Jesus said, "Blessed are ye, when men shall hate you, and when they shall separate you from their company, and shall reproach you, and cast out your name as evil, for the Son of man's sake. Rejoice ye in that day, and leap for joy: for, behold, your reward is great in heaven: for in the like manner did their fathers unto the prophets." (Luke 6:22-23 KJV)

When people "hate you" and "separate you from their company" because of your Christian beliefs, you will be *blessed.* You should "rejoice" and "leap for joy" when you are persecuted. You will be greatly rewarded in heaven for persevering in your commitment to Christ. Your Father wants you to look at everything that takes place in your life from an eternal perspective.

If you are criticized for your commitment to Christ, you should *rejoice* because you are absolutely certain that the Holy Spirit *is* in complete control and that He *will* take care of everything if you persevere in your commitment to Christ. "If you are censured and suffer abuse [because you bear] the name of Christ, blessed [are you – happy, fortunate, to be envied, with life-joy, and satisfaction in God's favor and salvation, regardless of your outward condition], because the Spirit of glory, the Spirit of God, is resting upon you…"(I Peter 4:14 AMP)

The first part of this verse of Scripture is similar to Luke 6:22 that we have just studied. I Peter 4:14 then goes on to explain *why* you should react with joy when you are persecuted for Christ. You should rejoice in the face of persecution because the Holy Spirit "is resting upon you." When you do, you provide the Holy Spirit with the opportunity to produce the spiritual fruit of joy in your life because you react to persecution with absolute commitment to Jesus Christ (see Galatians 5:22).

This chapter is filled with facts from the holy Scriptures explaining *why* you should react with joy *whenever* you face adversity for *any* reason. We pray that you will meditate on these facts from God's Word when you face adversity and particularly when you are persecuted because of your commitment to Christ.

Chapter 17

Thank God Instead of Complaining

You have seen many facts from the holy Scriptures that explain why you should have a constant attitude of gratitude toward Jesus Christ. What do you do if you are extremely grateful to another person? You thank that person.

You should thank Jesus continually for paying the *full* price for *all* of your sins. Your heartfelt gratitude should pour out of your mouth as you thank Jesus again and again for what He has done for you.

In this chapter we will look into the Word of God for facts and instructions about thanking the Lord. Before doing this, we first will look into the Bible for facts about the opposite of thanking the Lord – complaining.

You cannot experience the joy of the Lord when you complain. Complaining and joy do not go together. Complaining *blocks* the joy of the Lord from being manifested in your life. Your Father is not pleased if you complain. "…when the people complained, it displeased the LORD…" (Numbers 11:1 KJV)

Please highlight or underline the word "displeased" in this verse of Scripture. This verse refers to the Israelites complaining when they were in the wilderness. God was not pleased when the Israelites complained. Your Father is not pleased if He hears you complain.

If you have absolute faith in God, you will *not* complain. You must understand that you are complaining *against the Lord* when you complain. "…he has heard your grumbling against him. Who are we?

You are not grumbling against us, but against the LORD." (Exodus 16:8 NIV)

Please highlight or underline the words "against him" in this verse of Scripture. These words also refer to the complaints of the Israelites when they were in the wilderness. "Do all things without grumbling and faultfinding and complaining [against God]…" (Philippians 2:14 AMP)

Please highlight or underline the words "all things" in this verse of Scripture. These words include *whatever* you are tempted to complain about at any time, no matter how justified you may feel about your reason for complaining.

Please highlight or underline the words "against God" in the amplification of this verse of Scripture. Once again you are told that you actually are complaining *against God* whenever you complain. If you complain, you clearly indicate that you do not have absolute faith in God.

You are not perfect. You probably will complain from time to time. If you become aware that you have complained, go to your Father. Tell Him you are sorry that you have complained against Him. Repent of the sin of complaining. Ask your Father to forgive you and to give you a fresh new start. He will do this (see I John 1:9).

Instead of complaining about anything, you should thank God, regardless of what is taking place in your life. "At all times and for everything giving thanks in the name of our Lord Jesus Christ to God the Father." (Ephesians 5:20 AMP)

Please highlight or underline the words "at all times and for everything" in this verse of Scripture. Your Father does not leave any doubt as to how often He wants you to thank Him. Your Father wants you to thank Him continually, regardless of the circumstances you face.

When you face adversity you should look at this challenge as an opportunity to trust God because you know Him and you know His Word. You should not complain. You should thank God continually because you are certain that He always does exactly what He says He will do in His good timing. "...thanks be to God, which giveth us the victory through our Lord Jesus Christ." (I Corinthians 15:57 KJV)

In Chapter 7 you saw many facts from the Bible pertaining to the victory that Jesus Christ won for you. If you know these spiritual truths and if you truly believe that God does what He says He will do, you will thank God continually.

Jesus wants you to be certain that He is with you at all times and that He has won a total, complete and absolute victory. He wants you to live every day with a thankful heart because you are absolutely certain that God is in complete control. "...Give thanks to the Lord, for He is good; for His mercy and loving-kindness endure forever!" (Psalm 107:1 AMP)

Why are you instructed to "give thanks to the Lord?" You are instructed to thank the Lord because He is good. He is merciful. He loves you with an incredible love that is beyond the limits of your human comprehension. He is always kind to you. Thank Him and trust Him completely regardless of the circumstances you face.

We have explained that God often emphasizes through repetition. When God puts the exact same verse of Scripture in the Bible two different times, you can be certain that He is emphasizing whatever principle these two verses teach. The following verse of Scripture is exactly the same as Psalm 107:1. "...Give thanks to the Lord, for He is good; for His mercy and loving-kindness endure forever." (Psalm 136:1 AMP)

Many times seemingly severe adversity will turn into tremendous blessings *if* you react to adversity in obedience to God's specific in-structions, if you have absolute faith in God and if you thank Him continually. "Thank [God] in everything [no matter what the circum-stances may be, be thankful and give thanks], for this is the will of God for you [who are] in Christ Jesus [the Revealer and Mediator of that will]." (I Thessalonians 5:18 AMP)

Please highlight or underline the words "in everything" in this verse of Scripture. Please highlight or underline the words "no matter what the circumstances may be" in the amplification. Your Father once again instructs you to thank Him at *all times*, regardless of the circumstances you face.

You should not be worried and anxious when you face difficult circumstances. Instead, you should go to God in prayer. "Do not be anxious about anything, but in everything, by prayer and petition, with thanksgiving, present your requests to God. And the peace of God, which transcends all understanding, will guard your hearts and your minds in Christ Jesus." (Philippians 4:6-7 NIV)

Please highlight or underline the words "about anything" and "in everything" in this passage of Scripture. No matter what challenges you face, you should go to your Father in prayer. You should *thank Him when you pray.*

If you have absolute faith that your Father will answer your prayers, you will not wait to thank Him until after He has answered your prayers. If you refuse to be anxious and instead go to God in prayer, thanking Him as you pray, you will experience His peace that is so great that it "transcends all understanding." His peace will "guard *your* heart and *your* mind."

You must understand the absolute importance of thanking God when you pray. "Be earnest and unwearied and steadfast in your prayer [life], being [both] alert and intent in [your praying] with thanksgiving." (Colossians 4:2 AMP)

Your Father wants you to persevere in faith when you pray. He wants you to pray "with thanksgiving" each time you pray, regardless of how the circumstances look. "Offer to God the sacrifice of thanksgiving, and pay your vows to the Most High, and call on Me in the day of trouble; I will deliver you, and you shall honor and glorify Me." (Psalm 50:14-15 AMP)

Please highlight or underline the words "Offer to God" in this verse of Scripture. When you thank God, you are making an offering to Him, just as you make an offering when you put money in a collection plate at church.

Please highlight or underline the words "the sacrifice of thanksgiving" in this verse of Scripture. You should be sacrificial when you pray. Make the sacrifice to thank God as you have been instructed to do even if there does not appear to be any reason why you should thank Him.

Please highlight or underline the words "call on Me in the day of trouble" in this passage of Scripture. Always go to your loving Father in prayer when you are in trouble. Pray with faith. Thank Him. Rejoice. Honor Him. Glorify Him.

If you do these things, you can be certain that He will "deliver you." You will know that God has answered your prayer. You will be like the psalmist who said, "I will confess, praise, and give thanks to You, for You have heard and answered me..." (Psalm 118:21 AMP)

You can be certain that your Father *hears* your prayers. You can be certain that He will answer your prayers that are prayed with faith according to His will. (see John 15:7, I John 3:22 and I John 5:14-15).

In this chapter you have seen that your Father is not pleased when you complain. You have seen that you should thank God when you pray, before He answers. You have seen that He is pleased when you thank Him at all times because of everything He has done for you and because of your absolute faith in Him.

When you face adversity, you continually make a choice. You decide whether you will complain and feel sorry for yourself or whether you will rejoice and thank God because of your deep, strong and unwavering faith in Him. There is a definite relationship between living in the joy of the Lord and thanking God at all times.

Chapter 18

Praise the Lord Continually

In this chapter you will learn many facts from the Bible about praising the Lord. We would like to comment on the difference between praising the Lord and thanking the Lord. Many times the Scriptures treat praising the Lord and thanking the Lord exactly the same. You should thank the Lord continually for what He has done for you and what you are believing He will do in answer to your prayers.

Praising the Lord is similar to thanking the Lord, but praising the Lord often goes farther than thanking Him. You praise the Lord for what He has done for you and what you are believing Him to do in the future. You also should praise the Lord for *Who He is.* You praise the Lord to glorify Him for His magnitude and splendor. You should be like the psalmist who said, "...my mouth shall praise You with joyful lips" (Psalm 63:5 AMP)

Please highlight or underline the words "with joyful lips" in this verse of Scripture. These words explain the relationship between praising the Lord and having so much joy in your heart that the abundance of this joy flows out of your mouth as you praise Him (see Matthew 12:34).

Your praise is extremely important to God. He created you to praise Him. "The people I formed for Myself, that they may set forth My praise [and they shall do it]." (Isaiah 43:21 AMP)

If God created you for a specific purpose, shouldn't you focus on doing what God created you to do? God deserves your praise. Praise

Him continually. "Great is the LORD and most worthy of praise; his greatness no one can fathom." (Psalm 145:3 NIV)

Please highlight or underline the words "no one can fathom" in this verse of Scripture. You cannot even begin to understand the greatness of the Lord with the limitations of your human understanding. The Lord is *so great* that He is "*most worthy* of praise." Jesus Christ said, "…pay to God the things that are due to God." (Matthew 22:21 AMP)

You are blessed to have an opportunity to give something to God Who has given *so much to you*. As you grow and mature as a Christian, you will understand more and more how loving and compassionate your Father is. You will praise Him and thank Him often. "Oh, that men would praise [and confess to] the Lord for His goodness and loving-kindness and His wonderful works to the children of men! For He satisfies the longing soul and fills the hungry soul with good." (Psalm 107:8-9 AMP)

Your Father will satisfy the longing of your soul when you consistently give Him the praise that He so richly deserves. Unbelievers and some Christians do not have a deep desire to praise the Lord and thank Him. As you grow and mature and begin to comprehend how much the Lord has done for you and how great He is, you will praise Him and thank Him more. "…Give praise and thanks to the Lord of hosts, for the Lord is good; for His mercy and kindness and steadfast love endure forever!..." (Jeremiah 33:11 AMP)

Please highlight or underline the words "the Lord is good; for His mercy and kindness and steadfast love endure forever" in this verse of Scripture. Your Father is forever merciful, kind and loving. He will forgive all of your sins.

The more you worship, praise, thank and love the Lord, the more you will be filled with God Himself. You should thank the Lord and praise Him whether you feel like thanking Him and praising Him or not. You should be like the psalmist who said, "With a freewill offering I will sacrifice to You; I will give thanks and praise Your name, O Lord, for it is good." (Psalm 54:6 AMP)

Please highlight or underline the words "sacrifice to You" in this verse of Scripture. When you make a sacrifice, you go above and beyond anything that may be required of you. When you make a sacrifice of praise to the Lord, you forego anything else you would like to do to praise the Lord. "...let us offer the sacrifice of praise to God continually, that is, the fruit of our lips giving thanks to his name." (Hebrews 13:15 KJV)

Once again, please highlight or underline the word "sacrifice" in this verse of Scripture. When you feel the least like praising the Lord often is the time you should praise Him the most. Please highlight or underline the word "continually" in this verse of Scripture. Praise the Lord again and again.

Praising God is easy when everything is going well. You must understand the importance of praising God when you face adversity. Adversity should be a spiritual trigger that causes you to praise God. The more adversity you face, the more you should praise God and thank Him and rejoice.

If you have absolute faith that God will do everything His Word says He will do, you *will* praise Him continually, regardless of whether you feel like praising Him. When you praise God in the face of seemingly severe adversity, continual praise gives clear evidence of your deep, strong and unwavering faith in God.

When you praise the Lord, you are doing what angels do. Shortly before Jesus Christ was born in Bethlehem, an angel appeared before a group of shepherds to tell them about the birth of the Messiah.

The angel who made this announcement was joined by many other angels. They praised the Lord together. "Suddenly a great company of the heavenly host appeared with the angel, praising God and saying, 'Glory to God in the highest, and on earth peace to men on whom his favor rests.'" (Luke 2:13-14 NIV)

A vast multitude of angels praised the Lord on that first Christmas. Even though you cannot see the angels in the atmosphere around you, you can be certain that angels are there and that they are praising God continually. As you join these angels in continual praise, you unite yourself with them. You and God's angels become of one accord.

Praise is the language of heaven. Everyone in heaven is so exhilarated by God's presence that they praise Him continually. If you praise the Lord and worship Him continually, you will experience a preview of heaven while you are on earth.

Most Christians praise the Lord when they attend church. Your Father does not want you to limit your praise to the time you are in church. His Word instructs you to praise Him continually. "From the rising of the sun to the going down of it and from east to west, the name of the Lord is to be praised!" (Psalm 113:3 AMP)

You should praise the Lord from the first thing in the morning until the last thing before you go to sleep at night. Praising the Lord should be a way of life to you. You should be like the psalmist who said, "Seven times a day do I praise thee because of thy righteous judgments." (Psalm 119:164 KJV)

The number seven is a significant number in the Bible. This number means "complete." We believe that you will be blessed if you do your best to focus on praising the Lord *at least* seven times each day. Your Father instructs every one of His children to praise Him. "Let everything that has breath and every breath of life praise the Lord! Praise the Lord! (Hallelujah!)" (Psalm 150:6 AMP)

Please highlight or underline the words "everything that has breath" in this verse of Scripture. These words include *you*. Praising the Lord should be a way of life to you. Praise should be so much of an ingrained part of your life that you will praise God spontaneously on many occasions during each day and night.

When you praise the Lord, you focus on the Lord. Instead of thinking about yourself and the problems you face, you should praise the Lord. If you sincerely desire to see the joy of the Lord manifested in your life, you should faithfully obey your Father's instructions to praise Him continually, regardless of the circumstances in your life.

If you establish the delightful habit of consistently praising the Lord, you will be obeying your Father's instructions. You will be like the psalmist who said, "Why art thou cast down, O my soul? and why art thou disquieted in me? hope thou in God: for I shall yet praise him for the help of his countenance." (Psalm 42:5 KJV)

Please highlight or underline the words "cast down" and "disquieted" in this verse of Scripture. Do you sometimes feel that you have been cast aside and that no one cares about what you are going through? Are you agitated within yourself because of the difficult circumstances you face?

The psalmist asked himself *why* he felt this way. He did not give up hope. He praised the Lord because of his absolute faith that He would help him. If you praise the Lord continually in the face of adversity, your praise takes your focus off the problems you face and focuses your attention on the Problem Solver.

Praising the Lord is easy when the balance in your bank account is high, your health is good and everything else is going well. The real test of your faith in God comes when you praise the Lord continually even though everything that can go wrong seems to be going wrong.

You should praise the Lord just as heartily when you are in the depths of valleys as you do when you are on the peak of mountains. God will honor your continual praise. "Let the people praise thee, O God; let all the people praise thee. Then shall the earth yield her increase; and God, even our own God, shall bless us." (Psalm 67:5-6 KJV)

Please highlight or underline the words "all the people" in this passage of Scripture. These words include you. God instructs *everyone* to praise Him. Please highlight or underline the words "*Then shall the earth yield her increase.*" Consistent praise brings blessings from God. You should be like the psalmist who said, "I will call upon the LORD, who is worthy to be praised: so shall I be saved from mine enemies." (Psalm 18:3 KJV)

Your Father will deliver you from your enemies if you faithfully obey His instructions to praise Him often, regardless of the circumstances you face. "Bless our God, O peoples, give Him grateful thanks and make the voice of His praise be heard, Who put and kept us among the living, and has not allowed our feet to slip." (Psalm 66:8-9 AMP)

Please highlight or underline the words "has not allowed our feet to slip" in this passage of Scripture. Your Father will protect you if you continually thank Him and praise Him. You will experience "...beauty instead of ashes, the oil of joy instead of mourning, the garment [expressive] of praise instead of a heavy, burdened, and failing spirit" (Isaiah 61:3 AMP)

Your Father instructs you to praise Him if you have a "heavy, burdened and failing spirit." The Bible compares praise to a "garment." A garment covers your body. You are instructed to cover yourself with praise at all times, just as you are covered by the clothing you wear.

If you obey these instructions, God will give you His "beauty" and His "joy" instead of the "ashes" and the "heavy, burdened and failing spirit" that Satan's demons will try to put on you.

You will be cleansed and purified if you praise the Lord continually. "As the refining pot for silver and the furnace for gold [bring forth all the impurities of the metal], so let a man be in his trial of praise [ridding himself of all that is base or insincere; for a man is judged by what he praises and of what he boasts]." (Proverbs 27:21 AMP)

Impurities in silver and gold are removed by severe heat. This same principle applies when you face adversity. If you react to adversity by praising God continually, your reaction will show that you trust God completely. Continual praise will cause you to draw closer to God. Continual praise will cleanse and purify you.

This chapter is filled with scriptural instructions pertaining to praising the Lord. Now that you have these instructions as a solid foundation, you are ready to learn from God's Word exactly *how* to praise the Lord.

Chapter 19

Sing Praise to God

We now are ready to look into the Word of God to see what it says about *singing* praise to God. God always emphasizes through repetition. When you see the emphasis in the following verse of Scripture, you can be *certain* that your Father wants you to continually sing praises to Him. "Sing praises to God, sing praises! Sing praises to our King, sing praises!" (Psalm 47:6 AMP)

Your Father tells you *four times* in one short verse of Scripture that He wants you to sing praises to Him. Can there be any possible doubt that God wants you to sing praises to Him? He would not have emphasized this instruction if singing praises was not very important to Him. "…Is anyone glad at heart? He should sing praise [to God]." (James 5:13 AMP)

Is your heart filled with the joy of the Lord? If your heart is filled with joy, you *should* sing praise to God. You have learned that your Father wants your heart to be filled with joy regardless of the circumstances you face. You have seen that you should be deeply grateful to the Lord for Who He is and for all He has done for you.

If you have this deep gratitude, your heart will sing with joy. You will be like the psalmist David who said, "I will praise You, O Lord, with my whole heart; I will show forth (recount and tell aloud) all Your marvelous works and wonderful deeds! I will rejoice in You and be in high spirits; I will sing praise to Your name, O Most High!" (Psalm 9:1-2 AMP)

Are you very grateful to the Lord for Who He is and for all He has done for you? If you are, you will praise Him and thank Him. You will learn in Chapter 21 that you can live in the presence of Jesus now by continually singing songs of praise to Him.

Your Father has given you many blessings that you did not earn and do not deserve. The more you learn about God's marvelous grace, love and compassion, the more desire you will have to sing praises to Him. "Praise the Lord! For it is good to sing praises to our God, for He is gracious and lovely; praise is becoming and appropriate." (Psalm 147:1 AMP)

Please highlight or underline the words "it is good to sing praises to our God." When you consistently sing praise to God, you are doing what your Father wants you to do. The songs of praise that well up out of your heart will express your gratitude for His wonderful grace. "...making melody to God with [His] grace in your hearts." (Colossians 3:16 AMP)

Give God the praise He so richly deserves. Open your mouth to continually sing praises to Him. "Praise the Lord! For the Lord is good; sing praises to His name, for He is gracious and lovely!" (Psalm 135:3 AMP)

You should be like the psalmist David who said, "The Lord is my Strength and my [impenetrable] Shield; my heart trusts in, relies on, and confidently leans on Him, and I am helped; therefore my heart greatly rejoices, and with my song will I praise Him." (Psalm 28:7 AMP)

Please highlight or underline the words "The Lord is my Strength and my [impenetrable] Shield" in this verse of Scripture and the amplification. Do you believe that the Lord will give you His supernatural strength? Do you believe that He will protect you with a powerful spiritual Shield that cannot be penetrated by anyone or anything? If you believe these promises from God, you will trust Him completely.

Please highlight or underline the words "I am helped" in this verse of Scripture. If you are certain that the Lord will help you, you will rejoice continually. You will sing praise to Him.

Jesus Christ has given you a total, complete and absolute victory over every problem you will ever face (see John 16:33, Romans 5:17, Romans 8:37-39 and I John 4:5). If you are absolutely certain of this great spiritual truth, you *will* sing songs of joy to the Lord. "...Sing to the Lord, for He has triumphed gloriously and is highly exalted..." (Exodus 15:21 AMP)

If you consistently speak and sing words of praise, this fervent praise will overcome any temptation that you might have to be discouraged. You will be like the psalmist who said, "...I am poor, sorrowful, and in pain; let Your salvation, O God, set me up on high. I will praise the name of God with a song and will magnify Him with thanksgiving" (Psalm 69:29-30 AMP)

The psalmist said that he was "poor and sorrowful." Did he feel sorry for himself? Did he grumble, gripe and complain? He did not express any negative emotions. Instead, he sang praises to the Lord.

Your Father wants you to have this same attitude when you face adversity. Instead of focusing on the problems you face, you are instructed to praise God and thank Him. When you sing and rejoice in the face of adversity, you *release* your faith in God.

If your heart is filled with God's Word, your faith in God will not waver because of the circumstances you face. You will be like the psalmist who said, "My heart is fixed, O God, my heart is steadfast and confident! I will sing and make melody." (Psalm 57:7 AMP)

Please highlight or underline the words "My heart is fixed" and "my heart is steadfast and confident" in this verse of Scripture. These words show you the relationship between a confident heart and singing praises to God.

Your heart should be so full of God's Word that your faith in God is deep, strong and unwavering. Your heart should sing with joy, regardless of the circumstances you face. You should consistently sing praise to God because your faith in Him is much greater than the seeming severity of any adversity you face. "Then believed they his words; they sang his praise." (Psalm 106:12 KJV)

If you have deep faith in God and you believe the promises in His Word, you will express your faith in God by continually singing songs of praise, regardless of the circumstances you face. You will be like the psalmist who said, "O God, my heart is fixed (steadfast, in the confidence of faith); I will sing, yes, I will sing praises, even with my glory [all the faculties and powers of one created in Your image]!" (Psalm 108:1 AMP)

Please highlight or underline the words "my heart is fixed (steadfast, in the confidence of faith)" in this verse of Scripture and the amplification. If you have absolute faith in God, you *will* sing praises. You will be like the psalmist David who said, "...I have trusted, leaned on, and been confident in Your mercy and loving-kindness; my heart shall rejoice and be in high spirits in Your salvation. I will sing to the Lord, because He has dealt bountifully with me." (Psalm 13:5-6 AMP)

Do you have absolute confidence in God's "mercy and loving-kindness?" Has God "dealt bountifully" with you? If so, your heart will rejoice and you will sing to the Lord continually. Once again we want to emphasize that your faith in God will increase if you consistently open your mouth and sing songs of praise to Him that are solidly anchored upon His Word.

The Bible says that faith comes from *hearing* the Word of God (see Romans 10:17). When your ears hear your mouth continually singing songs of faith that are anchored upon God's Word, your faith in God will increase.

Songs of praise are so powerful in the spiritual realm that these songs of praise often move the hand of God. We see an example of this principle when the apostle Paul and a believer named Silas sat in a prison in Philippi with their hands and feet locked in stocks. These men joined together in praising the Lord in their dark and damp prison cell in the middle of the night.

In the natural realm they had no reason to praise the Lord. Everything that could have gone wrong seemed to be going wrong for them. They refused to give up their joy. They knew that Jesus Christ had won a total victory for them.

Paul and Silas sang for joy. God honored their faith in Him. "...about midnight, as Paul and Silas were praying and singing hymns of praise to God, and the [other] prisoners were listening to them, suddenly there was a great earthquake, so that the very foundations of the prison were shaken; and at once all the doors were opened and everyone's shackles were unfastened." (Acts 16:25-26 AMP)

What caused the earthquake and prison doors to open? The only clue in this passage of Scripture is that Paul and Silas were praying and praising God. Follow their example when you face adversity.

Satan and his demons do not want your heart to be filled with joy. They want you to have a heavy heart. They do not want to have to listen to songs of praise flowing out of your mouth. The fifteenth century German Christian leader, Martin Luther, once said, "The devil, the originator of sorrowful anxieties and restless troubles, flees before the sound of music almost as much as he does before the Word of God."

The Bible instructs you to speak God's Word and to sing God's Word when you face adversity. You should make Satan and his demons continually listen to you speaking the Word of God with deep faith in God and to listen to you happily singing songs that praise God and worship Him. Satan and his demons will *flee* if you do this consistently (see James 4:7).

We have just studied several passages of Scripture that instruct you to sing praises to the Lord. Now we are ready to look into facts pertaining to the music of the world and the music of the Lord. You should be very careful about the music you listen to. Jesus Christ said, "...Be careful what you are hearing." (Mark 4:24 AMP)

You should take full advantage of every opportunity to fill your ears with anointed Christian music. You should be very careful not to allow the music of the world to pour into your ears. Some of the music of the world may sound good, but worldly music leaves out the Lord. "They have lyre and harp, tambourine and flute and wine at their feasts, but they do not regard the deeds of the Lord..." (Isaiah 5:12 AMP)

You might like the sound of some worldly music, but the music of God sings about God and to God. Worldly music is a poor substitute for the music of God. Your Father has instructed you to turn away from the world (see James 4:4 and I John 2:15-16).

There has been a steady regression in the quality of worldly music in recent years. When we were in high school and college, the music of the world was pleasant even though it did not glorify God. The loud, blaring and discordant music that prevails in the world today is the opposite of what God intended music to be.

Much of what the world calls music today is only noise that is permeated with perversion, drugs, sex, violence and profanity. A great deal of the music of the world is filled with anger, sadness, despair and frustration. Much of the music in the world today mocks God. Christian music that is based on the Word of God is *filled with joy*.

The world has perverted the music that God intended to be used to praise Him into so-called "music" that actually glorifies Satan who is the god of this world (see II Corinthians 4:4) instead of glorifying God as music should. Music has great spiritual power, both for God and for Satan.

The music of the world can block you from experiencing the joy of the Lord. Christian music that is solidly based on the Word of God will increase your joy if you listen to it and sing it consistently. "It is a good and delightful thing to give thanks to the Lord, to sing praises [with musical accompaniment] to Your name, O Most High," (Psalm 92:1 AMP)

Please highlight or underline the words "with musical accompaniment" in the amplification of this verse of Scripture. These words refer to instruments such as harps and lyres that were prevalent when this verse was written. We have found that one of the most effective ways to sing praises to the Lord is to sing along with some of the magnificent recorded Christian worship music that is available today (see worship music websites such as gaither.com, integritymusic.com, maranathamusic.com and worshipmusic.com).

These and other recording ministries provide glorious Christian music that is solidly anchored on the Word of God. If you consistently listen to this anointed worship music, the joy of the Lord *will* rise up inside you. As you sing along with the worship music, your heart will rejoice because you will come into the presence of the Lord instead of focusing on whatever problems you face (see Psalm 100:1-2).

You can go on the internet and check out these sources of Christian music. These are just a few of the best sources we have found. We especially recommend Bill Gaither and his friends. In addition to continually listening to their CDs and cassette tapes, we enjoy watching their marvelous recorded music videos and DVDs. We thank Bill and Gloria Gaither for bringing the glory of God to our hearts and for filling our home with praise to God.

We often enjoy an anointed concert in our family room. We have come to know and love the Gaither singers and musicians. We have spent hundreds of precious hours praising and worshiping God with them.

You also can purchase an I-pod and fill it with praise and worship music. You can carry an I-pod or another recording device in your pocket to listen to praise and worship music often during the day and to sing along with it. If you spend a significant amount of time in your car, you should take full advantage of this time to listen to worship music and to sing your praises to God.

We have found that doing routine tasks such as opening mail, making organizational lists and paying bills are great times to sing praise to the Lord. You can sing praise to the Lord when you are taking a shower or getting dressed. If you have praise and worship music playing while you pay your bills, you will find that singing along with anointed worship music can change what once was a chore into an enjoyable experience.

One excellent time to sing praises to the Lord is during your daily exercise time. If you are a walker or a jogger, you can have praise music with you at all times. I (Jack) walk almost every day with our dog, J.C. (who is named for Jesus Christ). I have worship music playing every step of the way. I sing along with it. My daily exercise time is very enjoyable because of the combination of physical exercise and praising God.

We recommend developing the habit of playing praise and worship music continually and singing along with it. If you do, you will be obeying your Father's repeated instructions to sing praises to Him continually. "Let the saints be joyful in glory: let them sing aloud upon their beds." (Psalm 149:5 KJV)

Your Father wants your heart to sing with joy from the first thing in the morning until the time you go to bed at night. Your heart should be so filled with joy that you sing praises to God throughout the day and night. Even when you are lying in bed at night, you should sing praise to the Lord and rejoice.

Singing praise to the Lord should be a way of life to you. Praise and worship music has wonderful energizing qualities. Whenever you are tired or tempted to be discouraged, put on a good praise music CD or other recorded praise music and sing along with it.

You will find that singing along with anointed praise and worship music will lift you up and energize you. As you sing songs of praise that are based upon the holy Scriptures, you will release the supernatural spiritual power of the Word of God.

Do not hesitate to sing praises to the Lord if you are not a good singer. God is not interested in the quality of your singing. He is interested in your heart (see I Samuel 16:7). You may sing out of tune, but He will be delighted to hear you singing praises to Him, regardless of your ability. "Make a joyful noise unto the LORD, all the earth: make a loud noise, and rejoice, and sing praise. Sing unto the LORD with the harp; with the harp, and the voice of a psalm. With trumpets and sound of cornet make a joyful noise before the LORD, the King." (Psalm 98:4-6 KJV)

Please highlight or underline the words "all the earth" in this passage of Scripture. Once again your Father is instructing everyone in the world to sing for joy. Please highlight or underline the words "Make a joyful noise to the Lord." Your Father wants you to sing *loudly* to Him whenever you can. Your Father has instructed you to sing praise to Him along with musical accompaniment.

In Chapter 14 we mentioned research that was done by the University of Maryland School of Medicine on the relationship between laughter and good health. Michael Miller, MD, the principal investigator, said, "We had previously demonstrated that positive emotions such as laughter were good for vascular health. So the logical question was whether other emotions such as those evoked by music have a similar effect."

This group selected ten healthy non-smokers to participate in the study. These volunteers listened to recordings of their favorite music that they brought to the test. Blood vessel dilation tests showed conclusive positive reaction. The average upper arm blood vessel diameter increased 26% after the participants listened to the music of their choice.

This chapter has been filled with specific instructions from God about singing praises to Him. In the next chapter we will look into God's Word to study more instructions from God that will tell you exactly how you should release your praise to Him.

Chapter 20

How Excited Are *You* about the Lord?

Now that you have seen what the Word of God says about singing praise to God, we are ready to go one step further. In this chapter we will share with you several concepts that may seem controversial to you because they are so very different from the way that many Christians live.

We will back up each point that we make with Scripture. You will be able to decide for yourself whether these principles truly are controversial or whether what we are telling you is exactly what the Lord wants *you* to do, whether or not you have been doing any of these things in the past.

First, we will look into the holy Bible to see what your Father has to say about consistently raising your hands when you praise Him. You should follow the example of the psalmist David who said, "Because Your loving-kindness is better than life, my lips shall praise You. So will I bless You while I live; I will lift up my hands in Your name." (Psalm 63:3-4 AMP)

Your Father has been so loving and kind to you that you should praise Him and bless Him often. You should raise up your hands when you praise Him as an outward sign of your inward gratitude for everything He has done for you.

This passage of Scripture says that you *bless* God when you lift up your hands in His name. Perhaps you attend a church where people raise their hands when they praise the Lord. Perhaps this is not done in the church that you attend. "Lift up your hands in the sanctuary, and bless the LORD." (Psalm 134:2 KJV)

God's Word instructs you to "lift up your hands in the sanctuary." You will "bless the Lord" if you praise Him by doing what His Word instructs you to do. When you lift up your hands when you praise the Lord, you give an external manifestation of your love and adoration for Him. You should be like the psalmist who said, "My hands also will I lift up [in fervent supplication] to Your commandments, which I love..." (Psalm 119:48 AMP)

You should be so much in awe of the holy Bible that you actually praise God's Word. God said, "...this is the man to whom I will look and have regard: he who is humble and of a broken or wounded spirit, and who trembles at My word and reveres My commands." (Isaiah 66:2 AMP)

Please highlight or underline the words "trembles at My word and reveres My commands" in this verse of Scripture. Your Father wants you to be in awe of His supernatural living Word. He wants you to lift your hands and praise His Word just as you lift your hands and praise Him.

In the world when someone raises his or her hands before a police official, this action is a sign of surrender. When you lift up your hands before the Lord, you are making an outward manifestation of the inward surrender that is taking place in your heart.

When you raise your hands to the Lord, you give an outward indication that Jesus Christ is your Lord and Savior and that you have surrendered your life to Him. You should be like the psalmist who said, "I spread forth my hands to You; my soul thirsts after You like a thirsty land [for water]...." (Psalm 143:6 AMP)

When you consistently raise your hands to the Lord, you show the hunger and thirst that you have for a close and intimate relationship with Him. You should not wring your hands when you are tempted to be worried, concerned and afraid because of a seemingly severe problem. Instead, *lift* your hands in praise to the Lord as you praise Him and thank Him for the victory He has provided for you.

In addition to raising your hands as an outward manifestation of your praise to the Lord, the Bible also instructs you to *clap* your hands as a sign of your praise to the Lord. "Clap your hands, all you nations; shout to God with cries of joy. How awesome is the LORD Most High, the great King over all the earth!" (Psalm 47:1-2 NIV)

Please highlight or underline the words "all you nations" in this passage of Scripture. God wants everyone in the world to clap their hands and shout to Him with joy because they are in such awe of Him.

Jesus Christ won the greatest victory that has ever been won. He has made it possible for multitudes of sinful human beings to live eternally with Him in the awesome splendor of heaven. He has also made provision for you to live a victorious life here on earth.

Why wouldn't you clap your hands and shout for joy *if you truly believe* these great spiritual truths? You should have simple childlike faith in Jesus Christ. When little children are excited, their eyes light up and they clap their hands to express their joy. You should have this same childlike spontaneity in your life because of your absolute awe of what Jesus Christ has done for you.

God does not only instruct human beings to clap their hands before Him. His Word tells you that trees will clap their hands before Him. "…the mountains and the hills shall break forth before you into singing, and all the trees of the field shall clap their hands." (Isaiah 55:12 AMP)

Everything that God has created should worship Him. Mountains and hills should sing praise to the Lord. Trees should clap their hands. Mountains and hills do not have mouths. Trees do not have hands.

Some of the Bible is poetical, not literal. This figurative instruction from God shows you the emphasis that your Father places on every person clapping his or her hands in rejoicing to the Lord. "…let all those that put their trust in thee rejoice: let them ever shout for joy, because thou defendest them: let them also that love thy name be joyful in thee." (Psalm 5:11 KJV)

Please highlight or underline the words "all those" in this verse of Scripture. *Do you* trust the Lord completely? If you do, you should "rejoice." You should "shout for joy" because you are absolutely certain that God is defending you and protecting you.

You have seen examples of God's instructions pertaining to lifting your hands and clapping your hands when you praise Him. His Word contains additional instructions that tell you to shout for joy. "Let those who favor my righteous cause and have pleasure in my uprightness shout for joy and be glad and say continually, Let the Lord be magnified, Who takes pleasure in the prosperity of His servant." (Psalm 35:27 AMP)

Please highlight or underline the words "shout for joy and be glad" in this verse of Scripture. You should magnify the Lord continually. Your heart should be so filled with joy because of Who He is and all He has done for you that you will shout for joy in your exuberance.

Do *not* restrain your joy. *Let your joy come out.* Don't try to impress other people with your dignity. Impress your Father by continually praising Him and thanking Him and glorifying Him as you give Him the praise, honor and recognition He so richly deserves. "Let Your priests be clothed with righteousness (right living and right standing with God); and let Your saints shout for joy!" (Psalm 132:9 AMP)

If Jesus Christ is your Savior, you are righteous before God because Jesus has paid the price for all of your sins. You should do your very best to live a righteous life at all times. If you are continually conscious of your righteousness before God and if you are doing your very best to live a life that honors God, you will "shout for joy" because your heart is filled with joy. "Be glad in the Lord and rejoice, you [uncompromisingly] righteous [you who are upright and in right standing with Him]; shout for joy, all you upright in heart!" (Psalm 32:11 AMP)

The joy of the Lord should be so predominant in your life that you will shout for joy because you know you are righteous before Him and because you are absolutely certain that you will live throughout eternity with Him. You also should shout for joy because you are certain that the Lord is in complete control in every aspect of your life. "...the Lord our God the Omnipotent (the All-Ruler) reigns! Let us rejoice and shout for joy [exulting and triumphant]! ..." (Revelation 19:6-7 AMP)

God is omnipotent. He has all power (see I Chronicles 29:11-12). If you are absolutely certain that God has all power, regardless of the seeming severity of the problems you face, you *will* "rejoice and shout for joy." You will shout with a voice of triumph because you are absolutely certain that you are victorious over whatever problem you face. Persevere in your faith in God. Absolutely refuse to give up.

Some Christians say that they praise the Lord silently. This is *not* what the Word of God instructs you to do. Your Father instructs you to praise Him boldly by clapping your hands and shouting when you praise Him.

You must turn *away* from the world and the ways of this world. There is nothing wrong with shouting for joy. Refuse to allow any thoughts that you may have had before you read these instructions from God to influence you. If the holy Scriptures repeatedly instruct you to shout for joy, then go ahead and shout for joy. *Do* what God's Word repeatedly instructs you to do.

Hopefully you are a member of a church where praise to the Lord is celebrated by raising hands, clapping hands, singing and shouting to the Lord just as the Bible instructs us to do. Unfortunately, some churches today are somber places. Many people in these churches think it is undignified to raise their hands, clap their hands and shout for joy.

These people are doing exactly the opposite of what God's Word instructs them to do. God never meant for a church service to be somber. He has instructed individuals to praise Him and churches to worship Him in the sanctuary.

Many religious people attend church as a duty. They do not look forward to going. They count the time until the service ends. The stern, ritualistic and predictable services in some churches are not at all uplifting.

Somber churches with predictable and ritualistic services often are stagnant or decreasing in growth. In these difficult times, many churches that obey God's instructions to praise Him continually, to sing praises to Him, to worship Him, to raise hands, clap hands and shout for joy are experiencing rapid growth. People come into these churches and they sense the presence of the Lord. They will come back. They will bring their family members and friends.

Churches that are filled with the joy of the Lord open each service with praise and worship music. The presence of the Lord is obvious in these churches. The Bible clearly instructs you to thank God and praise Him when you attend church. "I will give thee thanks in the great congregation: I will praise thee among much people." (Psalm 35:18 KJV)

Even if you do attend a church that praises the Lord at every service, you should be very careful that you are not merely making a perfunctory expression of praise as you mouth the words of familiar songs. Praising the Lord should flow out of your heart that overflows with gratitude to Jesus Christ for His incomprehensible sacrifice on your behalf.

Some people get so used to praising the Lord in church that they just go through the motions. As they praise the Lord, they look around and observe what other people are wearing. They think where they will go after church. They may raise their hands and sing songs of praise, but their attention is elsewhere.

If you ever find that this is happening to you, we recommend that you *close your eyes* to shut out all distractions. Focus on the Lord. Do not just raise your hands and sing the words of familiar songs by rote. Think about what you are singing. Think about your gratitude to the Lord. Personalize your praise and worship to Him.

Self-centered people have a difficult time praising the Lord because their lives revolve around themselves instead of revolving around the Lord. Unbelievers and religious people feel uncomfortable when they are in the presence of Christians who exuberantly praise the Lord. They choose to believe that these exuberant Christians are wrong even though they are doing exactly what God's Word instructs them to do.

The flesh does not want to praise the Lord. Satan and his demons do not want you to praise the Lord continually. They know that consistent praise brings you into the presence of God and will cause them to flee. Satan and his demons will do everything they can to influence you against boldly praising the Lord.

All unbelievers and many religious people are spiritually dead within themselves regarding the ways of God. They cannot comprehend why they should praise the Lord continually. You must have a close and intimate relationship with God to praise Him continually.

Do not be concerned with what other people might think. You should be concerned about learning what your Father has instructed you to do. Faithfully obey the instructions He has given you regarding praise and worship and in every other area of your life.

People in the world do not think that people are strange when they go to an athletic contest and raise their hands, clap their hands and sing and shout for joy because their team is doing well. Many people get more excited because a team has moved a ball across a line, hit a ball over a fence or shot a ball through a hoop than they do about the greatest victory of all time that Jesus Christ won at Calvary.

If these people can get this excited about something that is happening with a ball, why can't *you* raise your hands and clap and shout and sing for joy for the greatest victory that has ever been won? No victory by any athletic team on earth can remotely compare to the magnificence of the victory that Jesus Christ won for you at Calvary.

Refuse to restrain your joy and excitement. Do what God's Word instructs you to do. Let yourself go. Consistently praise God and rejoice as you sing. Raise your hands, clap your hands and shout for joy.

What we are talking about here is not emotionalism. We are talking about obedience to specific instructions that your Father has given to you. If you consistently do what the Word of God has instructed you to do in your praise and worship, the emotions will come later. The emotions will be the *result*, not the cause.

You have learned that you should worship the Lord throughout every day and night of your life, not just when you are in church. If you have any hesitancy about doing what your Father has instructed you to do, we recommend that you begin by praising Him in privacy.

If possible, go to a room in your home where you can praise the Lord and do all of the things we have talked about in this chapter. Play some uplifting worship music. Praise God exuberantly along with this music.

If you don't have a place in your home where you can praise the Lord exuberantly, get in your car and drive with the windows closed and worship music playing. Sing loudly. Shout. Lift up your hands while you are waiting at a stop sign or traffic light.

No one is there to question your actions. If you begin doing these things in the privacy of your home or your car, we believe that you will be very surprised. The more you praise the Lord in this way, the more you will want to continue doing what God's Word has instructed you to do.

A healthy attitude of praising the Lord must be developed. The best way to learn how to praise the Lord and to worship Him is by praising Him and worshiping Him. At first, praise and worship may seem unnatural to you. The more you do what the holy Bible has instructed you to do in this area, the more natural and spontaneous your praise and worship will be.

When just you and the Lord are present, open your mouth and praise Him boldly. Thank Him for everything He has done for you. Praise Him in every way that you can for Who He is. If you will do this in privacy many times, you will get over any hesitancy you may have had about praising the Lord. You will be ready to praise Him boldly and publicly just as His Word has instructed you to do.

Chapter 21

Rejoice in the Presence of the Lord

Your heart *will* sing with joy if you have learned and faithfully obeyed the scriptural instructions that have been included so far in this book. You will find that this consistent attitude of joy actually will bring you into the presence of the Lord.

Stop and think for a moment about the awesome privilege of actually being able to come into God's presence. Could you pick up a telephone and call the president of the United States and immediately be invited into his office at the White House? Could you pick up a phone and call the governor of your state and immediately be able to come into his or her office? You know that you could not do these things, but you *are* able to contact the God Who created you, the president and the governor and come into His presence at any time.

The Creator of the universe yearns for you to come into His presence. Let's look again at a magnificent promise from God that we studied in Chapter 8. "Come close to God and He will come close to you..." (James 4:8 AMP)

God *wants* to come close to you. He *will* come close to you *if* you obey His specific instructions. Before Jesus Christ won the greatest victory of all time at Calvary, coming into the presence of God was a very complicated affair. Moses built a special tabernacle following specific instructions that God gave him. This tabernacle consisted of two rooms. The outer room was called the Holy Place. The inner room was called the Holy of Holies. A thick veil was placed between these two rooms to protect the Holy of Holies.

On one day each year after the Day of Atonement, a selected high priest was able to enter the tabernacle to come into the presence of God. When Jesus died on the cross, the veil was ripped from top to bottom. "…Jesus cried with a loud voice, and gave up the ghost. And the veil of the temple was rent in twain from the top to the bottom." (Mark 15:37-38 KJV)

We studied part of this verse of Scripture in Chapter 3 when we looked into the Bible for numerous facts pertaining to the crucifixion of Jesus Christ. We now are ready to look at the splitting of the veil in more detail in regard to coming into the presence of God.

No person is able to enter into the presence of God based upon his or her own worthiness. *You are made worthy* to come into God's presence by the shed blood of Jesus Christ that has cleansed you from all sin. Coming into God's presence is no longer limited to a high priest doing this one day each year.

If Jesus Christ is your Savior, you do not have to go through a priest, a minister or any other person. You have been given the magnificent opportunity to enter into God's presence 24 hours a day, 365 days a year. "…we have full freedom and confidence to enter into the [Holy of] Holies [by the power and virtue] in the blood of Jesus," (Hebrews 10:19 AMP)

Please highlight or underline the words "*full* freedom and confidence" in this verse of Scripture. The word "full" means total and complete. Because of the price that Jesus paid for you, there are *no* restrictions in regard to you coming into God's presence.

You should be in *absolute awe* that *you* actually have been given the privilege of entering into the presence of Almighty God. "Tremble, thou earth, at the presence of the Lord, at the presence of the God of Jacob" (Psalm 114:7 KJV)

Every Christian should tremble because of the awareness that he or she actually can come into the majestic presence of the God of the universe. "Honor and majesty are [found] in His presence; strength and joy are [found] in His sanctuary." (I Chronicles 16:27 AMP)

The presence of the Lord is majestic. You are privileged beyond all limits of human comprehension by actually being able to come into His presence. You will experience His supernatural strength and His joy when you are in His presence. "Humble yourselves [feeling very insignificant] in the presence of the Lord, and He will exalt you [He will lift you up and make your lives significant]." (James 4:10 AMP)

Please highlight or underline the words "Humble yourselves [feeling very insignificant] in the presence of the Lord" in this verse of Scripture and the amplification. You will understand how insignificant you are and how great He is when you are in His glorious presence. If you are humble because of this tremendous privilege you have been given, the Lord "will exalt you."

Please highlight or underline the words "He will lift you up and make your lives significant" in the amplification of this verse of Scripture. If you truly are humble in regard to the awesome privilege you have been given of coming into the presence of the Lord, He will honor your humility. He will do great things in you, through you and for you if you willingly acknowledge how insignificant you are and how great, awesome and majestic He is.

You should be eternally grateful to Jesus Christ for the enormous price He paid for you. Jesus has provided you with glorious eternal salvation. He also has provided tremendous blessings for you throughout your life on earth. You should sing songs of praise to Him continually. "O come, let us sing to the Lord; let us make a joyful noise to the Rock of our salvation! Let us come before His presence with thanksgiving; let us make a joyful noise to Him with songs of praise!" (Psalm 95:1-2 AMP)

The very best place that you can be is in the presence of the Lord. There is no place on earth that can even remotely compare to the joy of being in the presence of the Lord. Please highlight or underline the words "Let us come before His presence with thanksgiving" in this passage of Scripture.

In Chapter 17 you saw several passages of Scripture that instructed you to thank God continually, regardless of the circumstances you face. If you faithfully obey these instructions, your constant attitude of thanksgiving will bring you into His presence.

In Chapters 18 and 19 you saw many facts from the holy Bible about praising the Lord and singing praise to Him. If you consistently obey these instructions, you will experience the joy of coming into the glorious supernatural presence of the Lord. "Make a joyful noise to the Lord, all you lands! Serve the Lord with gladness! Come before His presence with singing!" (Psalm 100:1-2 AMP)

Please highlight or underline the words "all you lands" in this passage of Scripture. These words apply to every person on earth. You are here on earth to serve the Lord. You are instructed to serve Him "with gladness." You will experience great joy, meaning and fulfillment if you are faithfully carrying out the specific assignment that God has given to you.

Please highlight or underline the words "Come before His presence with singing" in this passage of Scripture. You saw many verses of Scripture pertaining to singing praises to God in Chapter 19. If you consistently obey these instructions, you *will* come into His presence. You come into God's presence through consistent praise and thanksgiving. "Enter into his gates with thanksgiving, and into his courts with praise: be thankful unto him, and bless his name." (Psalm 100:4 KJV)

If your heart is filled with gratitude, you will constantly thank the Lord for all that He has done. When you do, you will "enter into His gates." You then are told that you will enter "into his courts with praise." Thank God for all that He does. Praise Him for Who He is. A constant outpouring of praise and thanksgiving *will* bring you into God's glorious presence and keep you there.

When the Israelites praised God, their praise brought them into the holy place where God dwells. This same spiritual phenomenon applies to *you* today if Jesus Christ is your Savior. "...You are holy, O You Who dwell in [the holy place where] the praises of Israel [are offered]." (Psalm 22:3 AMP)

Know that God inhabits your praises. Faithfully obey His instructions to praise Him continually. Come into His presence repeatedly.

Everyone in heaven is filled with joy. You can experience a preview of heaven during the remainder of your life on earth if you learn how to come into the presence of the Lord by faithfully obeying the specific scriptural instructions that are contained in this book and additional instructions that are included in the Bible. "Blessed (happy, fortunate, to be envied) are those who dwell in Your house and Your presence; they will be singing Your praises all the day long...." (Psalm 84:4 AMP)

Please highlight or underline the words "dwell in Your house" in this verse of Scripture. When you dwell in a place, you live there permanently. Each time you come into God's presence, you will have a deep yearning to come into His presence even more.

Your Father wants you to grow and mature to the point where you will *remain* in His presence 24 hours a day, 7 days a week and 52 weeks a year. You will come into His presence and remain there if you sing praises to Him "all the day long." "Thou wilt shew me the path of life: in thy presence is fulness of joy; at thy right hand there are pleasures for evermore." (Psalm 16:11 KJV)

Please highlight or underline the words "fulness of joy" in this verse of Scripture. There is *no greater joy* than the joy that you will experience when you are in the presence of the Lord. If you faithfully obey God's instructions and praise Him and worship Him continually, you will experience "pleasures for evermore." No one can take your joy from you when you are in the presence of the Lord. "...You will enrapture me [diffusing my soul with joy] with and in Your presence." (Acts 2:28 AMP)

The word "rapture" means to be carried away with joy. The word "enrapture" means to be in the midst of this great joy. The word "diffused" means to be spread out or to be dispersed. Joy will fill your soul when you are in God's presence.

Your soul consists of your thoughts, your emotions and your will. Your thoughts will be filled with joy when you are in the presence of the Lord. You will constantly experience the emotion of joy. Every decision that you make when you are in the presence of the Lord will fill your heart with joy because you will know that you are doing exactly what your Father wants you to do. "...times of refreshing shall come from the presence of the Lord." (Acts 3:19 KJV)

You will be spiritually refreshed when you are in the presence of the Lord. You will not be pulled down by adversity because you will rest in the Lord. You will gladly give all of your burdens to Him because you trust Him completely. When you are in His presence, you will be certain that He can and will bring you safely through every challenge you face. "...the Lord said, My Presence shall go with you, and I will give you rest." (Exodus 33:14 AMP)

You should rest in the Lord at all times, faithfully giving your heavy burdens to Him (see Matthew 11:28-30). "Seek the Lord and His strength; yearn for and seek His face and to be in His presence continually!" (I Chronicles 16:11 AMP)

Please highlight or underline the words "yearn" and "continually" in this verse of Scripture. When you yearn for something, you have a deep desire for it. Your desire to be in God's presence should be the top priority in your life. Would your Father have instructed you to be in His presence *continually* if this were not possible? Very few Christians come into God's presence and remain there.

You should constantly "seek the Lord and His strength." Every aspect of your life should revolve around your desire to be in the presence of the Lord. "You have said, Seek My face [inquire for and require My presence as your vital need]. My heart says to You, Your face (Your presence), Lord, will I seek, inquire for, and require [of necessity and on the authority of Your Word]." (Psalm 27:8 AMP)

Please highlight or underline the words "Seek My face [inquire for and require My presence as your vital need]" in this verse of Scripture and the amplification. Being in the presence of the Lord is a "requirement." Being in the presence of the Lord is a "vital need." You must understand the vital importance of coming into God's presence and remaining there. You are told in the amplification of this verse of Scripture that you will be able to do this "on the authority of Your Word."

This book is filled with facts from the holy Bible that tell you exactly what to do to come into the presence of God and to remain there. If you study, learn and faithfully obey these specific instructions, you *will* rejoice continually because you will come into the presence of the Lord and remain there.

Chapter 22

Do Not Allow Satan to Steal Your Joy

There is no question that God wants every one of His children to rejoice continually. Satan always wants the opposite of what God wants. Satan and his demons will do everything they can to try to steal the joy of the Lord from you.

You saw in Chapter 9 that Satan and his demons are thieves. Their primary goal is to steal everything they can from every person they can (see John 10:10). You must not allow Satan and his demons to steal the joy that Jesus Christ paid such a great price to provide for you.

There is a definite relationship between the joy of the Lord and receiving the strength of the Lord (see Nehemiah 8:10). We will study this verse of Scripture in detail in a subsequent chapter.

Satan and his demons do not want you to receive strength from the Lord. They know that they can block you from receiving the Lord's strength in your life if they can steal the joy of the Lord from you.

Jesus wants you to be strong. Satan wants you to be weak. *You decide* throughout every day of your life whether you will give up your joy and be weak or whether you will absolutely refuse to give up your joy and receive strength from the Lord.

When you face adversity, Satan's demons will do everything they can to pull you into spiritual darkness. They know that they can steal your joy if you are in darkness. Your Father does not want you to allow Satan and his demons to pull you into spiritual darkness. He wants you to walk in His supernatural light. "…you were once darkness, but now you are light in the Lord. Live as children of light." (Ephesians 5:8 NIV)

Please highlight or underline the words "Live as children of light" in this verse of Scripture. You were in darkness before Jesus Christ became your Savior. When Jesus became your Savior, His light came into your life. Jesus wants you to live in His light throughout each day and night of your life.

You have seen that the Word of God instructs you to keep God first at all times and to thank Him continually because of your constant attitude of gratitude. If you disobey these instructions, you will allow Satan's demons to pull you into darkness. "…they knew and recognized Him as God, they did not honor and glorify Him as God or give Him thanks. But instead they became futile and godless in their thinking [with vain imaginings, foolish reasoning, and stupid speculations] and their senseless minds were darkened." (Romans 1:21 AMP)

Please highlight or underline the words "they did not honor and glorify Him as God or give Him thanks" in this verse of Scripture. These words describe exactly how Satan wants you to live. You will become "futile and godless" in your thinking if you do not obey God's instructions. Your mind will be "darkened" because you are not living the way your Father has instructed you to live.

All unbelievers walk in darkness. They do not understand that they are walking in darkness, but they are walking in darkness nevertheless. Unfortunately, some Christians live primarily in spiritual darkness because they either do not know how the Bible instructs them to live or they disobey God's instructions. Jesus said, "…I am the light of the world: he that followeth me shall not walk in darkness, but shall have the light of life." (John 8:12 KJV)

Please highlight or underline the words "shall not walk in darkness" in this verse of Scripture. If you faithfully obey God's instructions to renew your mind in the Bible each day and to meditate day and night on God's Word, you will learn how your Father wants you to live. If you faithfully obey His instructions, you will not walk in darkness. Satan's demons will not be able to steal the supernatural joy that Jesus Christ has provided for you.

You have learned that you will walk in the joy of the Lord if you keep Jesus first, place other people second and put yourself in last place. Satan's demons will do everything they can to try to get into your mind to influence you to focus on yourself. Selfish people cannot walk in the joy of the Lord. Whenever you put yourself in first place ahead of Jesus and ahead of other people, you will not experience the joy of the Lord.

Satan once was an archangel in heaven. All of his demons were angels in heaven. They fell from heaven because of pride (see Isaiah 14:12-15 and Revelation 12:9). Satan and his demons consistently will attempt to influence you to be proud and selfish just as they are.

Your Father wants you to live a humble and selfless life. You continually decide whether you will put Jesus first and keep Him first or whether you will put yourself first and give Satan's demons an opportunity to steal your joy.

Satan's demons also will try to steal your joy by attempting to influence you to focus on the problems you face instead of focusing on the Word of God and God's indwelling presence. You have learned that God's Word instructs you to focus on God at all times and *not* to focus on the circumstances you face, no matter how difficult they may seem (see Psalm 16:8-9).

If you allow Satan's demons to influence you to focus on the adversity you face, you will give up the joy of the Lord. Jesus Christ won a total, complete and absolute victory over Satan and every one of his demons. "…He is the Head of all rule and authority [of every angelic principality and power]." (Colossians 2:10 AMP)

Please highlight or underline the words "all" and "every" in this verse of Scripture and the amplification. There is no question that Jesus Christ has won a total victory over Satan and *all* of his demons. Jesus has given this victory to *you*. He said, "Behold, I give unto you power to tread on serpents and scorpions, and over all the power of the enemy: and nothing shall by any means hurt you." (Luke 10:19 KJV)

The words "serpents and scorpions" in this verse of Scripture refer to Satan and his demons. Jesus has given you the power to "tread on" Satan and his demons. Jesus has put Satan and his demons under your feet in the spiritual realm. Please highlight or underline the words "over *all* the power of the enemy" in this verse of Scripture. You must *not* allow Satan and his demons to steal this victory from you.

Satan and his demons have no power to steal your joy or anything else from you unless you allow them to deceive you. "Leave no [such] room or foothold for the devil [give no opportunity to him]." (Ephesians 4:27 AMP)

This verse of Scripture refers to giving Satan a foothold in your life when you are angry. The same principle applies to giving Satan and his demons a foothold in any other area of your life. Do *not* give Satan and his demons any foothold to steal the precious joy that Jesus Christ has given to you.

Throughout each day of your life, you decide whether you will believe and take action on the truth of God's Word or whether you will believe the lies of the devil and do what he wants you to do. This book is filled with truth from the holy Scriptures pertaining to the joy of the Lord. If you learn and obey God's instructions and learn and have absolute faith in God's promises, Satan and his demons will not be able to steal the joy of the Lord from you. "Submit yourselves therefore to God. Resist the devil, and he will flee from you." (James 4:7 KJV)

Please highlight or underline the words "Submit yourselves therefore to God" in this verse of Scripture. *How* do you submit to God? You submit yourself to God by setting aside time each day to be close to Him, talking with Him as you pray and listening to Him.

You submit to God by obeying your Father's instructions to fill your mind and your heart with His supernatural living Word. You submit to God by consistently learning and obeying the specific instructions He has given to you. You submit to God by learning the promises in His Word and having absolute faith in Him and in the magnificent promises He has given to you.

The only way that you can effectively resist the devil is to submit yourself to God. If you consistently submit yourself to God, Satan and his demons "*will* flee from you."

Satan and his demons are very persistent. They want to steal your joy. You should be more persistent than they are. When Satan's demons are hammering away at you with the thoughts they want to put into your mind, you must not accept these lying thoughts that always are exactly the opposite of what God's Word says.

Satan and his demons often will try to put "What if?" thoughts into your mind. They will constantly try to get you to think "What if this happens?" or "What if that happens?". Satan and his demons want to influence you to use your God-given power to visualize what they want you to visualize. We are instructed to "…refute arguments and theories and reasonings and every proud and lofty thing that sets itself up against the [true] knowledge of God; and we lead every thought and purpose away captive into the obedience of Christ (the Messiah, the Anointed One)" (II Corinthians 10:5 AMP)

The words "every proud and lofty thing that sets itself up against the [true] knowledge of God" in this verse of Scripture and the amplification refer to Satan and his demons. You are instructed to "*refute* the arguments and theories and reasonings" that they try to put into your mind. Instead of allowing the lies of Satan to obtain a foothold in your mind, you are instructed to "lead every thought and purpose away captive into the obedience of Christ (the Messiah, the Anointed One)."

You fight a battle every day of your life. Will you give Satan and his demons a foothold in your mind or will you reject the thoughts they attempt to put into your mind and bring all of your thoughts into obedience to the instructions you are given in the Word of God?

Mature Christians refuse to give up their joy. They are single-minded. They will not allow Satan and his demons to influence their thinking. "Let your eyes look right on [with fixed purpose], and let your gaze be straight before you." (Proverbs 4:25 AMP)

You should keep moving straight ahead. You must not allow any adversity you face or any temptations or thoughts that Satan's demons try to put into your mind to turn you away from focusing on

God. Your mind and your heart should focus continually on God, His Word and His indwelling presence

Satan and his demons have no spiritual authority over any person who has received Jesus Christ as his or her Savior. Satan's *only* hope is to attempt to deceive you. Satan and his demons cannot deceive you if your heart is filled to overflowing with the supernatural living Word of God. "…the word of God abideth in you, and ye have overcome the wicked one." (I John 2:14 KJV)

The words "the wicked one" in this verse of Scripture refer to Satan. How do you "overcome the wicked one?" You overcome Satan and his demons by consistently filling your heart with the Word of God.

You will walk continually in the victory that Jesus Christ has won for you if your heart is filled with the supernatural Word of God. Whenever Satan's demons try to put thoughts into your mind, the abundance of God's Word in your heart should pour out of your mouth (see Matthew 12:34).

You do not fight battles in the spiritual realm with guns, knives or any other worldly weapon. You fight battles in the spiritual realm *with your mouth*. You should be like the psalmist David who said, "…by the word of thy lips I have kept me from the paths of the destroyer." (Psalm 17:4 KJV)

The words "the destroyer" refer to Satan and his demons. You have learned that Satan's goal is to destroy you (see John 10:10). Satan and his demons *cannot* destroy you if the Word of God continually pours out of your mouth from a faith-filled heart. You should have so much of God's Word in your heart that every word you speak consistently lines up with the holy Scriptures.

Satan's demons want to hear words of discouragement, doubt and fear coming out of your mouth. God wants to hear His Word continually pouring out of your mouth.

Your Father wants you to know exactly what He has promised to do. He wants you to have absolute faith that He *will* do what He has promised to do in His way and in His good timing. He wants your words and actions to consistently indicate your absolute faith in Him and the promises He has given you in His Word.

In addition to constantly speaking God's Word, you have learned that you should praise God, thank Him and worship Him continually. You have learned that you should consistently sing praises to God.

Consistent praise and worship flowing out of your mouth will block Satan's demons from stealing your joy. They *will* flee when you speak the Word of God continually and thank God and praise Him, regardless of the circumstances you face. You should make Satan's demons listen to your mouth boldly speaking the Word of God and consistently praising and worshiping God. You are submitting to God if you do these things. Satan's demons *will* flee.

Praise is aggressive action in the spiritual realm. When you praise God in the face of adversity, you tell Satan's demons that you will not give in to their influence. You have learned that consistent praise brings you into the presence of God. Satan's demons must flee before the presence of God.

When you praise the Lord continually, you go on the offensive in the spiritual realm. You put Satan and his demons on the defensive where they should be.

This chapter is filled with facts from the holy Bible about not allowing Satan and his demons to steal the joy of the Lord from you. The next chapter contains several instructions from God's Word about not allowing the circumstances you face or the actions of other people to steal your joy.

You will learn that you must not pursue worldly attractions that provide no lasting joy or fulfillment. The joy that Jesus has provided for you is enormously important in your life. You must not allow Satan to steal this joy through any of the methods you have learned about in this chapter or to steal your joy by tempting you to pursue the counterfeits for joy that fill the world in these last days before Jesus Christ returns for His church.

Chapter 23

Refuse to Give Up Your Joy

Whenever you are faced with an adverse situation, *you make the choice* whether or not you will give up your joy. Many people give up their joy because they do not know what the Bible says about *not* giving up their joy. In this chapter you will learn from the holy Scriptures exactly what you should do when you are tempted to give up the joy of the Lord that was placed in you when you received Jesus Christ as your Savior.

Many people give up their joy because they face seemingly unfavorable circumstances. "The vine is dried up and the fig tree fails; the pomegranate tree, the palm tree also, and the apple or quince tree, even all the trees of the field are withered, so that joy has withered and fled away from the sons of men." (Joel 1:12 AMP)

This verse of Scripture speaks of farmers whose crops have failed. Please highlight or underline the words "joy has withered and fled away from the sons of men." When something withers, it shrinks and weakens. Just as the crop of a farmer can wither, your joy can wither and go away.

Many people in the world are happy when things are going well, but they give up their joy when they face adversity. Your Father does *not* want your joy to flee away. God is joy. He wants you to live in such a close relationship with Him that your connection with joy cannot be broken.

If Jesus Christ is your Savior, you can be certain that the supernatural joy of Jesus Christ lives in your heart (see John 15:11). His joy is resident within you. Give it full rein. If Jesus lives in you and you truly have yielded your life to Him, you will not give up your joy. You will hold tightly onto the joy of the Lord that has been given to you.

Instead of focusing on any circumstance that might tempt you to give up your joy, focus on God Who loves you with incredible love. Focus constantly on the indwelling presence of God Who is with you throughout every minute of your life. "Be strong, courageous, and firm; fear not nor be in terror before them, for it is the Lord your God Who goes with you; He will not fail you or forsake you." (Deuteronomy 31:6 AMP)

Please highlight or underline the words "Be strong, courageous, and firm" in this verse of Scripture. Refuse to give in to fear. Focus continually on "the Lord your God Who goes with you."

Please highlight or underline the words "He will not fail you or forsake you." You will *not* give up your joy because you *know* that God will not leave you. He is with you every step of the way.

In addition to not allowing the circumstances you face to cause you to give up your joy, you also must not allow other people to steal your joy, regardless of how they treat you. You should obey the instructions of Jesus Christ Who said, "…no one can take from you your joy (gladness, delight)." (John 16:22 AMP)

Jesus spoke these words to His disciples shortly before He was crucified. He knew that the disciples would miss Him, but one day they would be reunited with Him. He told them that they should not allow His crucifixion to steal their joy.

This same principle applies to you today. You must not allow any human being to steal the supernatural joy of the Lord from you. You are united with Jesus at all times because He lives in your heart.

Identify continually with Jesus and His indwelling presence and the scriptural facts pertaining to the magnificent victory He won for you. Refuse to react negatively to what other people say to you or do to you.

Your Father instructs you to love everyone *regardless* of how they treat you. "Never return evil for evil or insult for insult (scolding, tongue-lashing, berating), but on the contrary blessing [praying for their welfare, happiness, and protection, and truly pitying and loving them]. For know that to this you have been called, that you may yourselves inherit a blessing [from God—that you may obtain a blessing as heirs, bringing welfare and happiness and protection]." (I Peter 3:9 AMP)

Please highlight or underline the word *"never"* in this verse of Scripture. No matter what other people do to you, you always should respond with love. There is no such thing as righteous indignation for a Christian. If you truly yield your life to Jesus Christ, you will *not* become indignant because of how other people treat you.

You should obey the advice that Jesus gave when He said, "…love your enemies, treat well (do good to, act nobly toward) those who detest you and pursue you with hatred, invoke blessings upon and pray for the happiness of those who curse you, implore God's blessing (favor) upon those who abuse you [who revile, reproach, disparage, and high-handedly misuse you]. To the one who strikes you on the jaw or cheek, offer the other jaw or cheek also; and from him who takes away your outer garment, do not withhold your undergarment as well. Give away to everyone who begs of you [who is in want of necessities], and of him who takes away from you your goods, do not demand or require them back again. And as you would like and desire that men would do to you, do exactly so to them." (Luke 6:27-31 AMP)

These instructions seem almost impossible to obey when someone treats you in a deplorable manner. Jesus would not have instructed you to react in this way if this reaction was impossible.

How do you love other people who are difficult to love? The answer is that you do not try to love other people with your insufficient human love. You must understand that God gave you His supernatural love when Jesus Christ became your Savior. "…God's love has been poured out in our hearts through the Holy Spirit Who has been given to us." (Romans 5:5 AMP)

Please highlight or underline the words "God's love" in this verse of Scripture. If Jesus Christ is your Savior, you can be certain that the supernatural love of God has been placed into *your* heart. When you are tempted to give up your joy because of what other people attempt to do to you, meditate on this great spiritual truth.

If your human love is inadequate, you should be determined to love other people with God's supernatural love. Jesus said, "This is My commandment: that you love one another [just] as I have loved you. No one has greater love [no one has shown stronger affection] than to lay down (give up) his own life for his friends." (John 15:12-13 AMP)

Please highlight or underline the words "My commandment" in this passage of Scripture. Jesus did not merely suggest that you love other people. He has *commanded* you to love other people, regardless of how they treat you. "Let all bitterness, and wrath, and anger, and clamour, and evil speaking, be put away from you, with all malice: and be ye kind one to another, tenderhearted, forgiving one another, even as God for Christ's sake hath forgiven you." (Ephesians 4:31-32 KJV)

Negative emotions such as anger, bitterness, resentment and jealousy can rob you of the joy of the Lord. If you consistently focus on Jesus Christ Who lives in your heart, these negative emotions will not be able to prevail in your life.

Some people give up their joy because of what the driver of another automobile does, because of the weather, because their favorite athletic team lost, because they didn't catch any fish or play golf well. You will find that one of the most difficult times to keep your joy is when you are very tired. Do not be surprised if words that do not demonstrate the joy of the Lord come out of your mouth when you are exhausted.

Whenever you are tempted to give up the joy of the Lord for any reason, we encourage you to meditate often on the following verse of Scripture. "Be still, and know that I am God…" (Psalm 46:10 NIV)

Please highlight or underline the words "be still" in this verse of Scripture. Instead of allowing yourself to be agitated by whatever challenges you face, open your mouth and say again and again "Be still … Be still … Be still … Be still … Be still … Be still … Be still … Be still."

Why should you be still? You should be calm, quiet and confident because you *know* that Almighty God lives in your heart. "One God and Father of [us] all, Who is above all [Sovereign over all], pervading all and [living] in [us] all." (Ephesians 4:6 AMP)

Please highlight or underline the words "pervading all and [living] in [us] all" in this verse of Scripture. The word "pervade" means to be prevalent throughout. God is omnipresent. He is on His throne in heaven., He is spread out throughout every one of His children in the world at the same time, living in all of them.

Why would you ever give up your joy for any reason if you are absolutely certain that your Father, Almighty God, lives in your heart? He is much greater and much more powerful than any person or any problem you will ever face.

Focus continually on obeying your Father's instructions to be calm and quiet because you know that He lives in your heart and that He is in complete control of every circumstance in your life. You will find that consistently opening your mouth to instruct yourself to be still will help you to be calm and quiet whenever you are tempted to lose your joy.

Refuse to give up your joy if you do not receive what you are believing God for as soon as you think you should receive it. Keep on rejoicing and praising God and thanking Him. Persevere in faith. "…let us not lose heart and grow weary and faint in acting nobly and doing right, for in due time and at the appointed season we shall reap, if we do not loosen and relax our courage and faint." (Galatians 6:9 AMP)

The Bible is filled with promises telling you what God will do, but you are *never* told *when* God will do what He promises. You must "not lose heart and grow weary." You can be certain that God *will* honor your faith in Him in His way and in His good timing if you persevere in your faith, absolutely refusing to give up the supernatural joy He has given to you.

Chapter 24

Do Not Look for Joy in the World

In this chapter you will learn many truths from the Bible that will explain exactly what you should *not* do if you truly want to experience the joy of the Lord. We will look at many commonly held beliefs in the world about what produces happiness. We have repeatedly emphasized that the world's ways are very different from God's ways. You *cannot* receive lasting joy, fulfillment and meaning in your life from following any worldly method for pursuing happiness.

You will see throughout this chapter that anything that puts self in first place cannot produce the joy of the Lord. Self-centered people whose thoughts, words and actions revolve around themselves cannot possibly experience the joy of the Lord.

Anything that puts self first is motivated by pride. The Bible consistently teaches that pride separates you from God and blocks God from working in your life. Proud, selfish and self-centered people cannot receive the joy of the Lord (see Psalm 138:6, Proverbs 16:5 and 16:18, Jeremiah 9:23-24 and Matthew 23:12).

You should never glorify yourself in any way. Any glory that may come to you should be diverted to the Lord. "...Let him who boasts and proudly rejoices and glories, boast and proudly rejoice and glory in the Lord." (I Corinthians 1:31 AMP)

You *can* boast and proudly rejoice *if* you boast of the Lord and rejoice in the Lord. We will repeatedly emphasize that you must turn away from exalting yourself to experience the joy of the Lord. "...God sets Himself against the proud (the insolent, the overbearing, the disdainful, the presumptuous, the boastful)—[and He opposes, frustrates, and defeats them], but gives grace (favor, blessing) to the humble." (I Peter 5:5 AMP)

Please highlight or underline the words "God sets Himself against the proud" in this verse of Scripture. You obviously cannot experience the joy of the Lord if God is setting Himself against you.

Please highlight or underline the words "and He opposes, frustrates, and defeats them" in the amplification of this verse of Scripture. Can you imagine God Himself opposing you, causing you to become frustrated and defeating you? This is exactly what He does to people who are puffed up with pride. You can only experience the joy of the Lord if you are *humble*.

Satan and his demons are proud. They will try to tempt you to be proud and to pursue selfish goals that are the world's substitutes for the joy of the Lord. "…every person is tempted when he is drawn away, enticed and baited by his own evil desire (lust, passions)." (James 1:14 AMP)

Please highlight or underline the words "every person" in this verse of Scripture. These words include you. Satan will try to tempt you to pursue your "own evil desire (lust, passions)." Satan wants you to put yourself in first place. He wants you to pursue selfish goals in an attempt to be happy.

Selfish goals are those desires that feed your flesh or your ego. Many unbelievers are driven to be accepted and honored. They do not understand that, if they have totally surrendered their lives to Jesus Christ, they will receive the acceptance they crave.

We believe that our generation lives in the last days before Jesus Christ returns for His church. The Bible explains what many people in this generation are like. These people are "…lovers of sensual pleasures and vain amusements more than and rather than lovers of God." (II Timothy 3:4 AMP)

You must *not* make the mistake of pursuing "sensual pleasures and vain amusements." Many people are looking for joy in the wrong place. The joy of the Lord does not come from satisfying your senses.

The joy of the Lord will *not* come to you if you place your selfish desires ahead of your love for God. The joy of the Lord will only come to God's children who truly love their Father and do their very best at all times to learn and obey the specific instructions He has given to them in His Book of Instructions, the Bible.

We are *not* saying that Christians should never experience pleasure from the things of the world. There is nothing wrong with enjoying wholesome hobbies, but you will make a big mistake if you put the pursuit of *any* worldly pleasure ahead of your commitment to stay close to God and to devote your life to serving Him and helping others.

Please stop and think about the following question. Do you know anyone who is selfish who is truly happy? Any thinking person will understand that selfishness and happiness do *not* go together.

Every sin is rooted in selfishness. Can you think of one sin that is not rooted in selfishness? Selfish people are not in harmony with God. Only Christians who are unselfish can experience the joy that God reserves for His children who continually serve Him and serve others.

The joy of the Lord can only be experienced by turning away from the ways of the world and turning toward God. The Bible says that Satan is the god of this world (see II Corinthians 4:4 and I John 5:19). The ways of the world are strongly influenced by Satan and his demons who attempt to influence people to be selfish and self-centered instead of unselfish and God-centered.

Joy does not come from things. The American humorist and philosopher Will Rogers once said, "There is a law of life as strong as the law of gravity. If you want to live a happy, successful and fulfilled life, you must love people and use things, not use people and love things."

Any happiness that unbelievers experience by pursuing selfish desires never lasts. "...the joy of the godless and defiled is but for a moment" (Job 20:5 AMP)

Please highlight or underline the words "but for a moment" in this verse of Scripture. The Bible explains that the pleasures of the world only produce temporary happiness. The Bible speaks of "...the fleeting enjoyment of a sinful life." (Hebrews 11:25 AMP)

You will never experience true joy, meaning, fulfillment and satisfaction from the things of this world. You cannot experience the joy of the Lord from sensual pleasure. "The eye is not satisfied with seeing, nor the ear filled with hearing." (Ecclesiastes 1:8 AMP)

This verse of Scripture refers to the senses. You will not receive lasting satisfaction from anything that you can see or anything you can hear. The joy of the Lord comes from the inside out, not from the outside in. "...the heart of fools is in the house of mirth and sensual joy." (Ecclesiastes 7:4 AMP)

Please highlight or underline the words "the heart of fools" in this verse of Scripture. You will be *foolish* if you attempt to find joy from any sensual source that is outside of God's instructions in the Bible. People who attempt to find joy from the pleasures of this world are pursuing Satan's substitutes for the joy of the Lord. Self-centered people always will be unhappy sooner or later.

The happiness of the world puts self in first place. God's joy puts Jesus Christ in first place, other people in second place and yourself in last place. Jesus said, "...seek (aim at and strive after) first of all His kingdom and His righteousness (His way of doing and being right), and then all these things taken together will be given you besides." (Matthew 6:33 AMP)

Please highlight or underline the words "first of all" in this verse of Scripture. You must put God first. Then everything else will fall into place. You cannot experience God's blessings in your life if you consistently place anyone or anything ahead of God. "...not going your own way or seeking or finding your own pleasure or speaking with your own [idle] words, then will you delight yourself in the Lord, and I will make you to ride on the high places of the earth..." (Isaiah 58:13-14 AMP)

Please highlight or underline the words "not going your own way or seeking or finding your own pleasure" in this passage of Scripture. If you want to experience the joy of the Lord, you must "delight yourself in the Lord." If you put the Lord in first place where He belongs and keep Him there, He "will make you to ride on the high places of the earth."

When you serve God, He brings out your personality and anoints and empowers you. He opens doors for you and arranges divine appointments for you. Living for God truly is the highest journey you can ever take.

Chapter 14 explains the relationship between laughter, joy and good health. Your laughter should come from the joy of the Lord in your heart. Many people in the world laugh at the temporary pleasure they experience, but this laughter does not last. "Even in laughter the heart is sorrowful, and the end of mirth is heaviness and grief." (Proverbs 14:13 AMP)

Many people in the world who are laughing one day are sad the next day. Many people who experience temporary happiness in the world soon experience "heaviness and grief." You must not pursue the temporary ways of the world in your desire to experience joy, happiness, meaning and fulfillment in your life.

Chapter 25

Joy Does Not Come from Wealth

We now are ready to look into God's Word to see what it says about seeking happiness from pursuing wealth. Many people think that they would be happy if they had a lot of money. This thought is a lie from Satan.

You must *not* love money or the things that money can buy. "People who want to get rich fall into temptation and a trap and into many foolish and harmful desires that plunge men into ruin and destruction. For the love of money is a root of all kinds of evil. Some people, eager for money, have wandered from the faith and pierced themselves with many griefs." (I Timothy 6:9-10 NIV)

Please highlight or underline the words "temptation and a trap" in this passage of Scripture. Satan and his demons will try to tempt you to be led by greed. You must understand that the love of money will lead you into "many foolish and harmful desires that plunge men into ruin and destruction." The love of money always gives Satan and his demons a foothold in your life. People who look to money and possessions in a desire for happiness have "wandered from the faith and pierced themselves with many griefs."

We are *not* saying that God does not want you to be prosperous. Your Father *does* want you to be prosperous (see Joshua 1:8, Psalm 1:2-3, Psalm 112:1-3, Proverbs 10:22 and III John 2). God wants you to be prosperous by learning and obeying His specific instructions, not by being greedy and selfish and pursuing wealth the way that many people in the world do. Jesus Christ said, "Do not gather and heap up and store up for yourselves treasures on earth…" (Matthew 6:19 AMP)

Jesus was very explicit and clear in this statement. You must not place emphasis on the accumulation of money. You can be prosperous, but only if you keep God first at all times instead of placing your desire for wealth ahead of God in any way. If God does bless you financially, you should not be impressed by these temporal financial blessings. "…if riches increase, set not your heart on them." (Psalm 62:10 AMP)

Some people are so caught up with pursuing fame and fortune that they devote most of their time and energy toward achieving these temporal worldly goals. People who look to worldly wealth for joy and happiness will only experience whatever temporary happiness these worldly possessions give them. There are *no* heavenly rewards for achieving wealth on earth.

Can you imagine arriving in heaven and having God come to you saying, "Congratulations on becoming a multi-millionaire while you were on earth."? Jesus said, "…woe to (alas for) you who are rich (abounding in material resources), for you already are receiving your consolation (the solace and sense of strengthening and cheer that come from prosperity) and have taken and enjoyed your comfort in full [having nothing left to be awarded you]." (Luke 6:24 AMP)

Please highlight or underline the words "already are receiving your consolation" in this verse of Scripture. Jesus wants you to have an eternal perspective. Instead of pursuing temporary worldly pleasure from achieving wealth, Jesus instructs you to put God first instead of allowing money to be on the throne of your life.

Jesus said, "No one can serve two masters; for either he will hate the one and love the other, or he will stand by and be devoted to the one and despise and be against the other. You cannot serve God and mammon (deceitful riches, money, possessions, or whatever is trusted in)." (Matthew 6:24 AMP)

Please highlight or underline the words "deceitful riches, money, possessions, or whatever is trusted in" in the amplification of this verse of Scripture. If you put money or the possessions that money can buy ahead of God, you will look for your happiness in worldly wealth and possessions.

Some people have more money than they could ever spend and many possessions that they do not need. These people cannot experience the joy of the Lord *if* they allow their accumulated wealth and possessions to come ahead of the Lord. "Whoever loves money never has money enough; whoever loves wealth is never satisfied with his income. This too is meaningless. As goods increase, so do those who consume them. And what benefit are they to the owner except to feast his eyes on them?" (Ecclesiastes 5:10-11 NIV)

The more wealthy many people become, the more they pursue wealth. They are like a dog chasing its tail. The pursuit of wealth for selfish desires "is meaningless." You should only pursue wealth because you desire to use any excess wealth to serve the Lord and to help other people. Jesus said, "...Guard yourselves and keep free from all covetousness (the immoderate desire for wealth, the greedy longing to have more); for a man's life does not consist in and is not derived from possessing overflowing abundance or that which is over and above his needs." (Luke 12:15 AMP)

You should *guard* yourself against the temptation to be wealthy. You will *not* experience the joy of the Lord from pursuing wealth that is "over and above your needs." Jesus went on to explain this principle with a parable. "...The land of a rich man was fertile and yielded plentifully. And he considered and debated within himself, What shall I do? I have no place [in which] to gather together my harvest. And he said, I will do this: I will pull down my storehouses and build larger ones, and there I will store all my grain or produce and my goods." (Luke 12:16-18 AMP)

This wealthy man was perplexed about what to do with all of the money he had accumulated. He decided to build large storehouses to store the abundance of his harvest. He also decided to focus on the pursuit of pleasure. "...I will say to my soul, Soul, you have many good things laid up, [enough] for many years. Take your ease; eat, drink, and enjoy yourself merrily." (Luke 12:19 AMP)

God spoke directly to this rich man in regard to his decisions. "...God said to him, You fool! This very night they [the messengers of God] will demand your soul of you; and all the things that you have prepared, whose will they be? So it is with the one who continues to lay up and hoard possessions for himself and is not rich [in his relation] to God [this is how he fares]." (Luke 12:20-21 AMP)

Please highlight or underline the words "you fool!" in this passage of Scripture. You can only experience the joy of the Lord as the result of a close and intimate relationship with God. You *cannot* experience the joy of the Lord through storing up money for selfish use, accumulating worldly possessions and pursuing worldly pleasure.

Some Christians have fallen into the trap of believing what the world believes about pursuing fame, fortune and power. Many people believe that being wealthy will make them happy. The Bible repeatedly explains that this belief is wrong. "Come now, you rich [people], weep aloud and lament over the miseries (the woes) that are surely coming upon you." (James 5:1 AMP)

God is describing the rich person who is corrupt and fraudulent. He is speaking of rich people who feed every earthly lust upon themselves and abuse people along the way (see James 5:2-6).

This verse of Scripture speaks directly to wealthy people whose hearts embrace evil. Please highlight or underline the words "weep aloud and lament over the miseries (the woes) that are *surely* coming upon you" in this verse of Scripture and the amplification. God's Word teaches that people who pursue the wealth of the world and do not keep God in first place definitely *will* experience unhappiness and misery. The only question is when, not if.

Once again we want to emphasize that God *does* want you to prosper, but He does not want you to *ever* put the wealth of the world or the things that money can buy ahead of Him. Many people who have obtained worldly fame and fortune are miserable because they do not know God.

Now let's look at God's instructions to His children who obtain wealth. "As for the rich in this world, charge them not to be proud and arrogant and contemptuous of others, nor to set their hopes on uncertain riches, but on God, Who richly and ceaselessly provides us with everything for [our] enjoyment. [Charge them] to do good, to be rich in good works, to be liberal and generous of heart, ready to share [with others]," (I Timothy 6:17-18 AMP)

The Bible repeatedly says that you should *not* be proud and arrogant. You should *not* set your hopes on uncertain worldly riches. You have seen again and again that you should put God in first place and other people in second place. Wealthy people must put God first and keep Him first. They must be generous to people who are less fortunate than themselves.

We have made many statements in this chapter that will go directly against the beliefs of some people who are reading these words. Before you disagree with any of the statements we have made, go back and see for yourself that *every* statement is solidly anchored upon the holy Scriptures. You must not rationalize. You must be willing to turn away from any previously held beliefs that do not line up with the Word of God.

Chapter 26

Joy Comes from God's Will for Your Life

In the last two chapters you learned several things that you should *not* do if you sincerely desire to experience the joy of the Lord. In this chapter we will look into the holy Bible to see exactly what you are instructed to do to seek, find and carry out God's assignment for your life. You will experience joy, meaning and fulfillment if you live your life the way your Father created you to live.

God knew you intimately before He formed you in your mother's womb. The psalmist David knew that God had a specific plan for every day of his life before he was born. God had a specific plan for your life before He created you. David said, "Your eyes saw my unformed substance, and in Your book all the days [of my life] were written before ever they took shape, when as yet there was none of them." (Psalm 139:16 AMP)

If you have received Jesus Christ as your Savior, this decision brought you into a spiritual position where you are given the opportunity to seek, discern, find and carry out God's will for your life. "…we are God's [own] handiwork (His workmanship), recreated in Christ Jesus, [born anew] that we may do those good works which God predestined (planned beforehand) for us [taking paths which He prepared ahead of time], that we should walk in them [living the good life which He prearranged and made ready for us to live]." (Ephesians 2:10 AMP)

Please highlight or underline the words "do those good works which God predestined (planned beforehand) for us [taking paths which He prepared ahead of time]" in this verse of Scripture and the amplification. You can clearly see that your life was "recreated in Christ Jesus" so that you will be able to do exactly what God has planned for your life.

You should have a deep, fervent and sincere desire to seek, find and carry out God's assignment for your life. Jesus Christ paid an enormous price on the cross at Calvary so that you could devote your life to doing what He has called you to do. "…He died for all, so that all those who live might live no longer to and for themselves, but to and for Him Who died and was raised again for their sake." (II Corinthians 5:15 AMP)

Please highlight or underline the two times the word "all" is used at the beginning of this verse of Scripture. This word includes *you*. Jesus does not want you to devote your life to pursuing selfish desires. Jesus died so that you could live your life "for Him Who died and was raised again" for you.

Meditate on this verse of Scripture. Pray often asking God to reveal to you exactly what He has called you to do with your life. "…The God of our forefathers has destined and appointed you to come progressively to know His will [to perceive, to recognize more strongly and clearly, and to become better and more intimately acquainted with His will]…" (Acts 22:14 AMP)

Please highlight or underline the words "to come progressively to know His will" in this verse of Scripture. If you wholeheartedly seek God's assignment for your life, your Father will *progressively* reveal more and more of what He has called you to do.

When you do something progressively, you do whatever you are doing in stages. God usually will reveal His will for your life a little at a time. Your Father may show you the big picture of what He wants you to do at first. He then will reveal the details as time goes by if you consistently persevere in seeking His plan for your life.

Jesus Christ is your example in every area of life. Jesus said, "…I do not seek or consult My own will [I have no desire to do what is pleasing to Myself, My own aim, My own purpose] but only the will and pleasure of the Father Who sent Me." (John 5:30 AMP)

Jesus made it very clear that He did not come to earth to do what He wanted to do. Jesus knew that He came to earth to do God's will. You should have the same fervent desire to devote your life to doing what God has called you to do.

Focus constantly on your certainty that God lives in your heart. Have absolute faith that He will guide you every step of the way to do what He has called you to do. The Bible speaks of "...Him Who, by (in consequence of) the [action of His] power that is at work within us, is able to [carry out His purpose and] do superabundantly, far over and above all that we [dare] ask or think [infinitely beyond our highest prayers, desires, thoughts, hopes, or dreams]" (Ephesians 3:20 AMP)

Please highlight or underline the words "the [action of His] power that is at work within us" in this verse of Scripture and the amplification. *Know* that the mighty power of God is at work within *you*. Believe wholeheartedly that He will help you to "carry out His purpose" for your life.

Please highlight or underline the words "infinitely beyond our highest prayers, desires, thoughts, hopes, or dreams" in the amplification of this verse of Scripture. Do *not* limit God. Believe that He can and will use you to do great things for Him that are beyond the limits of your comprehension. "We are assured and know that [God being a partner in their labor] all things work together and are [fitting into a plan] for good to and for those who love God and are called according to [His] design and purpose." (Romans 8:28 AMP)

Please highlight or underline the words "God being a partner in their labor" in the amplification of this verse of Scripture. You can be "assured and know" that God is with you at all times and that He will cause everything to work out for the best if you love Him and if you are sincerely seeking His plan for your life.

Do you love God with all of your heart? *Are you* totally committed to seeking, finding and carrying out God's assignment for your life? If you can answer these two questions affirmatively, you can be *certain* that God will cause everything to work for good as you fervently seek to successfully complete the assignment He has given to you.

God created you in such a way that you will experience His joy to the fullest when you successfully carry out His plan for your life. Jesus explained this principle when He taught about a rich man who called his servants to carry out specific assignments.

One of these servants did an exceptional job for this man. His master said, "...Well done, you upright (honorable, admirable) and faithful servant! You have been faithful and trustworthy over a little; I will put you in charge of much. Enter into and share the joy (the delight, the blessedness) which your master enjoys." (Matthew 25:23 AMP)

Please highlight or underline the words "Enter into and share the joy" in this verse of Scripture. *You* will enter into and share the joy of the Lord if you faithfully do the little things that God has called you to do with your life. If you devote yourself to successfully doing every little detail that God has given to you, you will experience great joy. God then will give you more important assignments.

You should be very committed to doing what God has called you to do. "Look carefully then how you walk! Live purposefully and worthily and accurately, not as the unwise and witless, but as wise (sensible, intelligent people), making the very most of the time [buying up each opportunity], because the days are evil. Therefore do not be vague and thoughtless and foolish, but understanding and firmly grasping what the will of the Lord is." (Ephesians 5:15-17 AMP)

This passage of Scripture implores you to *not* waste your time doing things that have no eternal significance. We live in the last days before Jesus Christ returns. You should be "making the very most of the time" you have remaining to seek, find and carry out God's will for your life.

The apostle Paul faced many severe obstacles, but he refused to allow any of these obstacles to overcome him. Paul said, "...none of these things move me; neither do I esteem my life dear to myself, if only I may finish my course with joy and the ministry which I have obtained from [which was entrusted to me by] the Lord Jesus..." (Acts 20:24 AMP)

Please highlight or underline the words "with joy" in this verse of Scripture. Paul did *not* give up his joy when he faced formidable obstacles as he pursued the assignment that Jesus had given him. Paul was determined to finish his course with joy by doing what Jesus was trusting him to do with his life.

Jesus wants you to experience great joy as you carry out His assignment for your life, regardless of the circumstances you face. He said, "Blessed (happy—with life-joy and satisfaction in God's favor and salvation, apart from your outward condition—and to be envied) are you who hunger and seek with eager desire now, for you shall be filled and completely satisfied!..." (Luke 6:21 AMP)

Please highlight or underline the words "you shall be filled and completely satisfied" in this verse of Scripture. You *will* experience the joy of the Lord to the highest degree if you hunger and thirst to seek, find and carry out His will for your life.

You have learned that the joy of the Lord is *not* dependent on the circumstances you face. You can be certain that you will experience great joy, meaning and fulfillment in your life if you are in the center of God's will and if you persevere with faith to successfully complete the assignment you have been given.

If you have faithfully obeyed your Father's instructions to renew your mind in His Word each day and to meditate day and night on the holy Scriptures, your mind and your heart will be filled with God's supernatural living Word. God's Word gives His general will for the lives of all of His children.

If your heart is filled to overflowing with God's Word, you will have programmed yourself in such a way that the Holy Spirit will use God's Word in your heart to reveal His assignment for your life. You will be like the psalmist David who said, "I delight to do thy will, O my God: yea, thy law is within my heart."(Psalm 40:8 KJV)

The life of Dr. Albert Schweitzer is a good example of a godly man who dedicated his life to serving God and other human beings. Dr. Schweitzer turned away from the worldly riches he could have received as a successful surgeon. He went into the African jungle where he spent his life helping lepers.

Dr. Schweitzer said, "The only ones among you who will really be happy are those who have sought and found how to serve. The interior joy we feel when we have done a good deed, when we feel we have been needed somewhere and have lent a helping hand is the nourishment the soul requires."

Dr. Schweitzer knew that he was called to utilize the gifts and talents that God gave him to serve Him and other people. He spoke of "really being happy," appropriating "inner joy" and receiving "the nourishment the soul requires." These words will apply to you if you are completely committed to doing what God has called you to do with your life.

John Wesley was an eighteenth century British theologian who founded the Methodist church. He traveled on horseback throughout Great Britain, usually preaching two or three times a day.

John Wesley once said, "Do all the good you can by all the means you can, in all the ways you can, in all the places you can, to all the people you can for as long as ever you can." He emphasized the importance of doing your very best at all times and in all places to serve every possible person.

Martin Luther was another Christian leader who understood the definite relationship between seeking, finding and carrying out God's will and experiencing the joy of the Lord. He said, "Blessed is he who submits to the will of God; he can never be unhappy."

You learned in Chapter 24 that you should not selfishly pursue happiness. The joy of the Lord does not come when you pursue it. Joy comes when you pursue God's will for your life.

When you eagerly seek to live your life in direct obedience to God's plan, you will experience the great joy that your Father has reserved for His children who devote their lives to carrying out the assignment He has given them. "...try to learn [in your experience] what is pleasing to the Lord [let your lives be constant proofs of what is most acceptable to Him]." (Ephesians 5:10 AMP)

God has given you specific gifts and talents so that you can serve Him and help others. God created you in such a way that you will experience joy to the fullest by ministering to others. As you give of the talents that God has given to you, God always will give back to you. "…whatsoever good thing any man doeth, the same shall he receive of the Lord…" (Ephesians 6:8 KJV)

Your Father wants you to be totally committed to seeking, finding and carrying out His assignment for your life. For additional facts from the holy Bible pertaining to God's will for your life, we recommend our Scripture Meditation Cards and the accompanying CD that are titled *Find God's Will for Your Life.*

Chapter 27

Joy Comes from Obedience

You have just read about the relationship between experiencing joy, meaning and fulfillment and being in the center of God's will for your life. In this chapter we will look into the relationship between obedience to God, consistent prayer and receiving God's joy in your life.

People who do not know much about the holy Bible often think that the instructions in God's Word are difficult to obey. This belief is incorrect. "…these orders of His are not irksome (burdensome, oppressive, or grievous)." (I John 5:3 AMP)

Please highlight or underline the words " *not* irksome" in this verse of Scripture. When something "irks" you, it irritates or annoys you. God's instructions are *not* irritating in any way. Please highlight or underline the words "burdensome, oppressive, or grievous" in the amplification of this verse of Scripture. Obedience to God's instructions is *not* a burden in any way.

Your Father has given you instructions for your own good. God's children who faithfully study and meditate on His Word and learn and obey His instructions will live a full life because God blesses obedience. Disobedience often blocks your loving Father from giving you the blessings He would like to give you.

There is a definite relationship between joy and obedience. God has given you many specific directions in His Book of Instructions, the Bible. If you learn everything you can about how your loving

Father instructs you to live and if you faithfully obey His instructions, you will have a sense of peace, security and joy deep down inside of yourself.

The more you learn about God's instructions and obey these instructions, the more joyous you will become. "You love righteousness and hate wickedness; therefore God, your God, has set you above your companions by anointing you with the oil of joy" (Psalm 45:7 NIV)

You will "love righteousness" as you learn more and more instructions from God. You will have a deep and strong desire to live your life in obedience to your Father's instructions. You will "hate" to live a life of disobedience. If you do your best at all times to learn and obey your Father's instructions, your Father will "anoint you with the oil of joy." Jesus said, "If you know these things, blessed and happy and to be envied are you if you practice them [if you act accordingly and really do them]." (John 13:17 AMP)

Please highlight or underline the words "act accordingly and really do them " in the amplification of this verse of Scripture. You must do more than just know what the Bible instructs you to do. You must "practice" God's instructions by living in obedience to them. "...he who keeps the law [of God, which includes that of man]—blessed (happy, fortunate, and enviable) is he." (Proverbs 29:18 AMP)

Please highlight or underline the words "blessed (happy, fortunate, and enviable) is he" in this verse of Scripture and the amplification. You will be blessed and happy if you obey God's instructions *and* the laws of the government in the town or city, state or province and country where you live.

God blesses obedience. Satan and his demons will do everything they can to attempt to influence you to not learn and obey God's instructions and to disobey the government's laws. You consistently decide throughout every day of your life whether you will be humble and obedient or proud and disobedient. If you are a humble and obedient child of God, your Father will bless you with His supernatural joy. "...let the [uncompromisingly] righteous be glad; let them be in high spirits and glory before God, yes, let them [jubilantly] rejoice!" (Psalm 68:3 AMP)

Please highlight or underline the words "[uncompromisingly] righteous" in this verse of Scripture and the amplification. If you are uncompromisingly righteous, you are righteous before God because the shed blood of Jesus Christ has paid the full price for yours sins. You should do your very best at all times to live a righteous life in obedience to the instructions of God.

If you do, you will "be glad." You will be "in high spirits." You will "jubilantly rejoice." Your Father has repeatedly assured you that you will be filled with joy if you learn and faithfully obey the specific instructions He has given to you. "...No good thing will He withhold from those who walk uprightly." (Psalm 84:11 AMP)

Please highlight or underline the words "walk uprightly" in this verse of Scripture. These words mean that you live your life in obedience to God's instructions. If you do, your heart will sing with joy because your Father will not withhold any good thing from you. "If they obey and serve Him, they shall spend their days in prosperity and their years in pleasantness and joy." (Job 36:11 AMP)

Once again the Bible shows that there definitely is a correlation between obeying God and experiencing joy. Please highlight or underline the words "If they obey and serve Him" in this verse of Scripture. Your Father wants you to obey the instructions He has given you in His Book of Instructions, the Bible.

He wants you to serve Him by seeking, finding and carrying out His assignment for your life. If you consistently obey God and serve Him, you will spend your days "in prosperity" and your years "in pleasantness and joy."

You have learned that God emphasizes through repetition. Your Father repeatedly promises that your life *will* be filled with joy if you consistently learn and faithfully obey His instructions.

Jesus said, "If you keep My commandments [if you continue to obey My instructions], you will abide in My love and live on in it, just as I have obeyed My Father's commandments and live on in His love. I have told you these things, that My joy and delight may be in you, and that your joy and gladness may be of full measure and complete and overflowing." (John 15:10-11 AMP)

Children show their love for their parents by obeying them. You show your love for your heavenly Father by obeying His instructions (see I John 5:1-3).

Please highlight or underline the words "abide in My love and live on in it" in this passage of Scripture. If you obey the instructions of Jesus Christ, you will live in His love just as He lived in His Father's love throughout His earthly ministry.

Please highlight or underline the words "My joy and delight may be in you" in this passage of Scripture. The joy and delight of Jesus Christ *will* fill your heart if you faithfully obey His instructions. Your joy will be "of full measure and complete and overflowing."

Your Father will give you joy if you are consistently dedicated to learning and obeying His instructions and if you devote your life to seeking, finding and carrying out His will for your life. "…to the person who pleases Him God gives wisdom and knowledge and joy…" (Ecclesiastes 2:26 AMP)

There is no question that there is a definite relationship between experiencing the joy of the Lord and obeying God's instructions. We will devote the rest of this chapter to studying God's Word to learn that your Father also will give you joy if you learn how to pray according to His instructions and consistently obey these instructions. "…the prayer of the upright is his delight." (Proverbs 15:8 KJV)

You are "upright" before God if Jesus Christ is your Savior. Your Father is delighted when you come to Him in prayer. Do you want your Father to be pleased with you? If so, you should learn how to pray effectively (see the 19 Scripture references on the topic of prayer on pages 343-351 of our book titled *What Does God Say?*).

You learned in Chapter 21 about the supernatural joy that you will experience when you are in the presence of God. Your heart will be filled with joy if you truly understand the *precious privilege* you have been given of going directly to the throne of God when you pray. You have been given the opportunity to go directly to the Creator of the universe to talk with Him at any hour of the day or night.

You have learned that your Father consistently instructs you to put Him and other people ahead of yourself. This principle applies to your prayer life. You can pray for yourself, but we believe that the majority of your prayers should be for other people. "…the Lord turned the captivity of Job and restored his fortunes, when he prayed for his friends; also the Lord gave Job twice as much as he had before." (Job 42:10 AMP)

Please highlight or underline the words "when he prayed for his friends" in this verse of Scripture. Anyone who has studied the life of Job knows that Job faced many problems. However, God restored Job's fortune and gave him "twice as much as he had before" *when he prayed for his friends.*

Self-centered people either do not pray or they pray primarily for themselves. When you pray, you should pray as Paul prayed for the Philippians. Paul said, "In every prayer of mine I always make my entreaty and petition for you all with joy (delight)." (Philippians 1:4 AMP)

When you pray for other people, you should pray "with joy (delight)." You should be excited about the privilege you have been given to go directly to the throne of God as you intercede for these needy people. Jesus Christ told you exactly how you should pray when He said, "If you live in Me [abide vitally united to Me] and My words remain in you and continue to live in your hearts, ask whatever you will, and it shall be done for you." (John 15:7 AMP)

Please highlight or underline the words "ask whatever you will, and it shall be done for you" in this verse of Scripture. Jesus promises to answer your prayers for other people and yourself *if* you meet specific conditions.

First, you must abide continually in Jesus Christ. Every aspect of your life should revolve around Him. This relationship is *vital.* Second, your heart should be filled with the Word of God. When you pray to God, your prayer requests should be solidly anchored upon specific promises from the holy Bible.

If you obey these instructions and you pray with absolute faith in God, you will rejoice because you will know that your Father will answer your prayers, just as Jesus said He would. "…whatsoever we ask, we receive of him, because we keep his commandments, and do those things that are pleasing in his sight." (I John 3:22 KJV)

Please highlight or underline the words "because we keep his commandments, and do those things that are pleasing in his sight" in this verse of Scripture. Your Father promises to answer *all* of your prayers *if* you obey His instructions by living the way He instructs you to live. "…this is the confidence that we have in him, that, if we ask any thing according to his will, he heareth us: And if we know that he hear us, whatsoever we ask, we know that we have the petitions that we desired of him." (I John 5:14-15 KJV)

Do you want to be *absolutely certain* that God hears your prayers? Do you want to be *absolutely certain* that God answers your prayers? This passage of Scripture tells you that God *does* listen to your prayers whenever you "ask any thing according to his will." God's will and God's Word are the same.

Please highlight or underline the two times the word "know" is used in this verse of Scripture. When you pray according to God's will and in obedience to His specific instructions, your heart will be *filled with joy* because you will be *certain* that God hears you and that He answers your prayers.

Your Father does not want you to wish, hope and beg when you go to Him in prayer. He wants you to pray based upon specific promises in His Word. He wants your heart to be filled with joy because you are absolutely certain that He always does exactly what His Word says He will do. "…The earnest (heartfelt, continued) prayer of a righteous man makes tremendous power available [dynamic in its working]." (James 5:16 AMP)

Please highlight or underline the words "earnest (heartfelt, continued) prayer" in this verse of Scripture and the amplification. Your Father wants you to pray earnestly from your heart on a continual basis. If you do, your prayers will "make tremendous power available." Your heart *will* sing with joy if you are absolutely certain that the mighty power of God will be released because of your fervent prayers.

The word "continued" in the amplification of this verse of Scripture is very important. Jesus urges you to persevere in your prayers, absolutely refusing to give up. He said, "…ask and keep on asking and you will receive, so that your joy (gladness, delight) may be full and complete." (John 16:24 AMP)

Please highlight or underline the words "ask and keep on asking and you will receive" in this verse of Scripture. Persevere in your prayers. Please highlight or underline the words "so that your joy (gladness, delight) may be full and complete" in this verse of Scripture and the amplification. Jesus spoke these words to His disciples during the Last Supper that He had with them before His crucifixion. Jesus did not want His disciples to give up when He was crucified. He wanted them to keep on praying.

These instructions also apply to you. If you are absolutely certain that God *will* answer your prayers that are solidly anchored upon His Word, your heart will be filled with joy, whether or not you already have received His answer.

This chapter is filled with facts from the Word of God about the relationship between experiencing the joy of the Lord, faithfully obeying God's instructions and persevering in prayer with absolute faith that God answers. We pray that these truths from the holy Bible will fill your heart with joy and encouragement.

Chapter 28

Joy Comes from Serving

You have learned in the last several chapters of the absolute importance of putting the Lord ahead of yourself. You cannot experience the joy of the Lord if you allow anyone or anything to come ahead of the Lord in your life. Jesus Christ said, "…Love the Lord your God with all your heart and with all your soul and with all your mind" (Matthew 22:37 NIV)

Please highlight or underline the *three times* the word "all" is used in this relatively short verse of Scripture. God always emphasizes through repetition. Jesus definitely emphasizes the importance of loving God ahead of everything else in your life.

Every aspect of your life should revolve around the Lord. If He truly is in first place in your life at all times, you *will* experience His supernatural joy. "…happy (blessed, fortunate, prosperous, to be envied) are the people whose God is the Lord!" (Psalm 144:15 AMP)

Please highlight or underline the words "happy (blessed, fortunate, prosperous, to be envied) in this verse of Scripture and the amplification. These words describe God's promise to *you*. God *will* do His part. Will you do your part? God emphasizes that this wonderful blessing is for "the people whose God is the Lord."

We have previously explained that you can only experience the joy of the Lord if you keep Jesus Christ in *first place*, other people in second place and yourself in last place. The best way to understand this spiritual principle is by the following vertical explanation of the word joy.

J – Jesus Christ first

O – Other people second

Y – Yourself last

People who do not experience the joy of the Lord do not keep Jesus Christ in first place. They do not place other people ahead of themselves. You can only experience the joy of the Lord to the degree that you humble yourself before Him and before others. Many people need to change the emphasis in their lives from "I, I, I" and "Me, Me, Me" to "Jesus, Jesus, Jesus" and "Others, Others, Others."

You cannot experience the joy of the Lord unless you put yourself in last place and keep yourself there. True joy, meaning and fulfillment in life come from serving God and serving others with the gifts, talents and energy that God has given to you.

Jesus Christ, Who came down from heaven to pay an incomprehensible price so that you would not have to suffer eternally in the lake of fire, should be your Savior. Jesus *also* should be the Lord of every day of your life. You should do what John the Baptist did when he said, "He must increase, but I must decrease. [He must grow more prominent; I must grow less so.]" (John 3:30 AMP)

Can you sincerely say that Jesus is growing more important in your life and that you are growing less important? Every aspect of your life should revolve around your absolute certainty that the victorious Jesus Christ lives in your heart and that He is with you throughout every minute of every hour of your life. "…from Him and through Him and to Him are all things. [For all things originate with Him and come from Him; all things live through Him, and all things center in and tend to consummate and to end in Him.] …" (Romans 11:36 AMP)

Please highlight or underline the words "all things" in this verse of Scripture. *Everything* that any person on earth is searching for can be found in Jesus Christ. You cannot experience true joy, meaning and fulfillment in your life unless every aspect of your life revolves around Jesus Christ Who is the Source of all things. "…I saw the Lord constantly before me, for He is at my right hand that I may not be shaken or overthrown or cast down [from my secure and happy state]." (Acts 2:25 AMP)

Please highlight or underline the words "my secure and happy state" in the amplification of this verse of Scripture. You *will* be secure and happy and no challenges that you face will be able to overcome you *if* you focus continually on the Lord and His indwelling presence. Your heart will rejoice if you are absolutely certain that your precious Lord is with you at all times. You can be certain that He *will* help you when you trust Him completely and persevere in your faith in Him (see Hebrews 2:18, 4:16 and 13:6).

Patrick Henry, who made the famous statement, "Give me liberty or give me death" in 1775 also said, "My most cherished possession I wish I could leave you is my faith in Jesus Christ, for with Him and nothing else you can be happy, but without Him and with all else you will never be happy."

These words that Patrick Henry spoke line up perfectly with the Word of God. You do not need anything except Jesus Christ to be filled with joy, meaning and fulfillment. You cannot experience true joy, meaning and fulfillment without Jesus.

There is a direct relationship between experiencing joy, meaning and fulfillment in your life and fearing the Lord. When you fear the Lord, you hold Him in reverent awe at all times. Every aspect of your life revolves around Him. "The Lord is near to all who call upon Him, to all who call upon Him sincerely and in truth. He will fulfill the desires of those who reverently and worshipfully fear Him; He also will hear their cry and will save them." (Psalm 145:18-19 AMP)

Please highlight or underline the two times the word "all" is used in this passage of Scripture. God's holy Word is speaking to *you.* If you have a deep and sincere desire for a close and intimate relationship with the Lord, you will fear Him by holding Him in reverent awe at all times.

Please highlight or underline the words "He will fulfill the desires" in this passage of Scripture. The Lord *will* give you fulfillment and meaning in your life if you truly do revere Him. "Serve the Lord with reverent awe and worshipful fear; rejoice and be in high spirits with trembling [lest you displease Him]." (Psalm 2:11 AMP)

Please highlight or underline the words "Serve the Lord with reverent awe and worshipful fear" in this verse of Scripture. Every aspect of your life should revolve around your deep and sincere reverence for the Lord. You *will* rejoice and be in high spirits if you truly revere the Lord.

Please highlight or underline the words "lest you displease Him" in the amplification of this verse of Scripture. If you sincerely desire to please the Lord, you will revere Him. You will have a deep and sincere desire to learn and obey His instructions. "Blessed (happy, fortunate, to be envied) is everyone who fears, reveres, and worships the Lord, who walks in His ways and lives according to His commandments. For you shall eat [the fruit] of the labor of your hands; happy (blessed, fortunate, enviable) shall you be, and it shall be well with you." (Psalm 128:1-2 AMP)

Please highlight or underline the word "everyone" in this passage of Scripture. This word includes *you*. If you fear the Lord at all times and hold Him in reverent awe and do your very best to serve Him and to obey His instructions, you *will* experience His joy in your life. If you truly fear the Lord, "it shall be well with you."

God's Word repeatedly emphasizes the relationship between His joy and humbling yourself before Him and before other people. "Do nothing from factional motives [through contentiousness, strife, selfishness, or for unworthy ends] or prompted by conceit and empty arrogance. Instead, in the true spirit of humility (lowliness of mind) let each regard the others as better than and superior to himself [thinking more highly of one another than you do of yourselves]." (Philippians 2:3 AMP)

Please highlight or underline the words "the true spirit of humility" in this verse of Scripture. If you truly look at other people as being superior to yourself, you will be filled with joy because you will be doing exactly what God has instructed to do. You truly will regard other people "as better than and superior to" yourself. "Let each of you esteem and look upon and be concerned for not [merely] his own interests, but also each for the interests of others." (Philippians 2:4 AMP)

God created a vacuum inside of you when He created you. This vacuum *cannot* be filled with selfish desires. Joy, meaning and fulfillment are only available to Christians who keep Jesus Christ and other people ahead of themselves at all times. Jesus said, "…everyone who exalts himself will be humbled (ranked below others who are honored or rewarded), and he who humbles himself (keeps a modest opinion of himself and behaves accordingly) will be exalted (elevated in rank)." (Luke 14:11 AMP)

Please highlight or underline the word "everyone" in this verse of Scripture. Jesus was speaking to *you* when He said that you "will be humbled" if you exalt yourself. You "will be exalted" if you consistently place other people ahead of yourself. "The meek also shall increase their joy in the LORD…" (Isaiah 29:19 KJV)

The word "meek" in this context means to be humble. You will *increase* your joy in the Lord *if* you truly have a servant's heart that is completely devoted to serving the Lord and helping other people. We have repeatedly emphasized that God's ways are *very* different from the ways of the world. You often will find joy and whatever else you seek in the opposite place from where your carnal nature wants to look.

True joy comes from giving, not from receiving. Jesus said, "…It is more blessed (makes one happier and more to be envied) to give than to receive." (Acts 20:35 AMP)

Please highlight or underline the words "makes one happier" in the amplification of this verse of Scripture. You *will* experience God's blessings of happiness and joy if you focus on giving instead of receiving. God's supernatural joy is reserved for His children who devote their lives to serving Him and to giving to others.

Immature people want to receive continually. Mature Christians know that they should focus on helping other people. "…[we ought to help carry the doubts and qualms of others] and not to please ourselves." (Romans 15:1 AMP)

Satan's demons will continually try to influence you to believe that you will experience happiness by pleasing yourself. Please highlight or underline the words "*not* to please ourselves" in this verse of Scripture. *Forget yourself.* Encourage other people and help them in any way you can. "...as we have opportunity, let us do good to all people, especially to those who belong to the family of believers." (Galatians 6:10 NIV)

Please highlight or underline the words "do good to *all* people" in this verse of Scripture. You should always be committed to doing everything you can to help every person you can. You are instructed to be especially aware of the needs of other Christians. Your sole purpose for being on earth is to serve God and to help others in every way you can, particularly your brothers and sisters in Christ.

Chapter 29

Joy from Yielding to the Holy Spirit

The Holy Spirit Who lives in the heart of every person who has received Jesus Christ as his or her Savior can and will help you to live in joy when you face adversity. "May the God of your hope so fill you with all joy and peace in believing [through the experience of your faith] that by the power of the Holy Spirit you may abound and be overflowing (bubbling over) with hope." (Romans 15:13 AMP)

Please highlight or underline the words "fill you with all joy and peace in believing [through the experience of your faith]" in this verse of Scripture and the amplification. You can clearly see the relationship between your faith in God and being filled with joy and peace through the Holy Spirit.

Please highlight or underline the words "that by the power of the Holy Spirit you may abound and be overflowing (bubbling over) with hope." The Holy Spirit will help you to persevere without giving up hope.

The Holy Spirit will flood your heart with hope *if* your faith in God is deep, strong and unwavering. Throughout every day of your life, you will constantly make the decision whether you will choose to control your own life or whether you will gladly surrender control of your life to the Holy Spirit Who lives in your heart. These decisions will depend on how much you trust in the Holy Spirit and His mighty power.

Your Father wants you to consistently make the quality decision to turn away from the desire to control your life and to decide to yield control of your life to the Holy Spirit. Your heart will be filled with joy *if* you can even begin to comprehend the magnitude of the power of the Holy Spirit and *if* you yield control of your life to Him because you trust Him completely.

You are headed for major problems if you are in control of your life. The only question is when you will experience adversity, not if. Jesus Christ wants to be more than your Savior. He wants to be the Lord of every hour of every day of your life. You will experience His supernatural joy if you gladly surrender every aspect of your life to Him and consistently praise Him and thank Him for doing in you and through you what you cannot do yourself.

We studied Galatians 2:20 in Chapter 10. We will look at this verse of Scripture again from the perspective of yielding control of your life to Jesus Christ Who lives in your heart. You should be like the apostle Paul who said, "I have been crucified with Christ [in Him I have shared His crucifixion]; it is no longer I who live, but Christ (the Messiah) lives in me; and the life I now live in the body I live by faith in (by adherence to and reliance on and complete trust in) the Son of God, Who loved me and gave Himself up for me." (Galatians 2:20 AMP)

Paul shared in the crucifixion of Jesus Christ when he willingly died to selfish desires by giving up control of his life to Jesus. Please highlight or underline the words "it is no longer I who live, but Christ (the Messiah) lives in me" in this verse of Scripture and the amplification. *Know* that you are not meant to be in control of your own life. *Why* would you ever attempt to control your life if you are absolutely certain that the victorious Jesus Christ lives in your heart?

Please highlight or underline the words "I live by faith in (by adherence to and reliance on and complete trust in) the Son of God" in this verse of Scripture and the amplification. Jesus loves you so much that He gave up His life for you. He has taken up residence in your heart if He is your Savior. "May Christ through your faith [actually] dwell (settle down, abide, make His permanent home) in your hearts!..." (Ephesians 3:17 AMP)

Please highlight or underline the words "through your faith" in this verse of Scripture. *Do you* have deep, strong and unwavering faith that Jesus Christ "makes His permanent home in your heart?" "…the Lord is the Spirit, and where the Spirit of the Lord is, there is freedom. And we, who with unveiled faces all reflect the Lord's glory, are being transformed into his likeness with ever-increasing glory, which comes from the Lord, who is the Spirit." (II Corinthians 3:17-18 NIV)

In the world many people think that they are free when they are doing what they want to do. Many years ago a popular song was titled "I Did It My Way." Satan wants you to do it your way. Satan and his demons will do everything they can to influence you to try to control your own life.

Please highlight or underline the words "there is freedom" in this passage of Scripture. You must understand that true freedom in the spiritual realm comes from the last place that unbelievers and immature Christians expect to find freedom. True freedom *comes from surrender.*

You will be "transformed" into the likeness of Jesus Christ if you yield control of your life to the Holy Spirit. "…live and move not in the ways of the flesh but in the ways of the Spirit [our lives governed not by the standards and according to the dictates of the flesh, but controlled by the Holy Spirit]. For those who are according to the flesh and are controlled by its unholy desires set their minds on and pursue those things which gratify the flesh, but those who are according to the Spirit and are controlled by the desires of the Spirit set their minds on and seek those things which gratify the [Holy] Spirit." (Romans 8:4-5 AMP)

Please highlight or underline the words "live and move *not* in the ways of the flesh but in the ways of the Spirit" in this passage of Scripture. Your life should *not* be controlled by your limited human abilities. Please highlight or underline the words "controlled by the Holy Spirit" in the amplification of this passage of Scripture.

You are an imperfect human being. You should constantly yield control of every aspect of your life to the mighty Holy Spirit Who lives in you. If the Holy Spirit truly is in control of your life, you will be living the way your Father wants you to live.

Your heart will be filled with joy if you are certain that God has given you the ability of the Holy Spirit to do in you, through you and for you what you cannot do yourself. You will live your life exactly the way that God wants you to live *if* the Holy Spirit is in control of your life. "…you are living the life of the Spirit, if the [Holy] Spirit of God [really] dwells within you [directs and controls you]…." (Romans 8:9 AMP)

Please highlight or underline the words "directs and controls you" in the amplification of this verse of Scripture. Nothing in the world is more meaningful, fulfilling and exciting than to have your life directed and controlled by the Holy Spirit. If you meditate on the Scripture references in this chapter, you will consistently yield more and more control of your life to the Holy Spirit.

Your heart will overflow with joy if you trust the Holy Spirit completely. You will willingly give up control of your life because of your absolute faith in Him and His supernatural ability and power. "If we live by the [Holy] Spirit, let us also walk by the Spirit. [If by the Holy Spirit we have our life in God, let us go forward walking in line, our conduct controlled by the Spirit.]" (Galatians 5:25 AMP)

Please highlight or underline the words "our conduct controlled by the Spirit" in the amplification of this verse of Scripture. If the Holy Spirit truly is in control of your life, you will live in joy. If you give up your joy, this action clearly indicates that you are in control of your life. Many Christians struggle and become frustrated *because they are in control of their lives.*

If you truly want to experience the joy of the Lord in your life, you must get out of the driver's seat. You will block the joy of the Lord from being manifested in your life if you attempt to do God's work for Him. You must trust the Holy Spirit completely to do in you and through you what you cannot do yourself.

You must not attempt to carry heavy burdens that your Father never intended for you to carry. "Commit your way to the Lord [roll and repose each care of your load on Him]; trust (lean on, rely on, and be confident) also in Him and He will bring it to pass." (Psalm 37:5 AMP)

Please highlight or underline the words "each care of your load on Him" in the amplification of this verse of Scripture. *Stop* trying to carry heavy burdens that the Lord does not want you to carry. Rejoice because you are absolutely certain that Jesus Christ lives in your heart. Rejoice because you know that He *will* bring you safely through every problem you will ever face as you yield to Him and trust in Him.

You will block Jesus from moving in your life if you struggle and strain, trying to make things happen yourself. Jesus will move in your life to the exact degree that you let go and trust Him instead of trying to do everything yourself. If you attempt to carry heavy burdens yourself, you will make a bad situation worse.

God has given you the right to control your life. If He did not, every person that He created would be a robot. "...O Lord, You are our Father; we are the clay, and You our Potter, and we all are the work of Your hand." (Isaiah 64:8 AMP)

You will live a full, balanced and complete life if you allow God to shape you and mold you. This verse of Scripture teaches that God is the "Potter" and that you are "the clay." Allow God to shape you and mold you by willingly yielding control of your life to Him.

The Book of Acts contains several accounts of the disciples of Jesus Christ being filled with the Holy Spirit after Jesus ascended into heaven. These disciples, who were used to depending completely on Jesus Christ, were *continually filled with joy* when they yielded control of their lives to the Holy Spirit.

You also will be filled with joy and filled with the Holy Spirit if you trust the Holy Spirit so much that you gladly yield control of your life to Him. "...do not get drunk with wine, for that is debauchery; but ever be filled and stimulated with the [Holy] Spirit. Speak out to one another in psalms and hymns and spiritual songs, offering praise with voices [and instruments] and making melody with all your heart to the Lord" (Ephesians 5:18-19 AMP)

Please highlight or underline the words "ever be filled and stimulated with the [Holy] Spirit" in this passage of Scripture and the amplification. Every aspect of your life should revolve around the mighty Holy Spirit Who lives in your heart. You must not allow yourself to be tempted by Satan's substitutes for the Holy Spirit – drunkenness and the constant pursuit of worldly pleasure.

Some people attempt to experience a temporary high by getting drunk. Getting drunk will not produce joy. Please highlight or underline the word "debauchery" in this passage of Scripture. The word "debauchery" is used here to refer to extreme indulgence in the pursuit of sensual pleasure.

This indulgence will separate you from the Holy Spirit Who will bless you abundantly if every aspect of your life is "filled and stimulated" with Him. The word "ever" in this passage of Scripture means always. You should speak the Word of God continually. You should sing songs of praise "making melody with all your heart to the Lord."

Obeying these instructions is all part of yielding control of your life to the Holy Spirit. "...the kingdom of God is not a matter of [getting the] food and drink [one likes], but instead it is righteousness (that state which makes a person acceptable to God) and [heart] peace and joy in the Holy Spirit. He who serves Christ in this way is acceptable and pleasing to God and is approved by men." (Romans 14:17-18 AMP)

Many people pursue the pleasures of the world in an attempt to find happiness. They often go out to dinner at luxurious restaurants and drink alcoholic beverages. If you truly want to experience the joy of the Lord, you will find that this supernatural joy comes from the inside out, *not* from any external source.

Please highlight or underline the words "[heart] peace and joy in the Holy Spirit" in this passage of Scripture and the amplification. You will experience the peace and joy of God in your life to the degree that the Holy Spirit truly is in control of your life. "...the fruit of the [Holy] Spirit [the work which His presence within accomplishes] is love, *joy (gladness)*..." (Galatians 5:22 AMP)

Galatians 5:22-23 lists all of the fruit that will be experienced in your life when the Holy Spirit truly is in control. Since we are focusing on the subject of joy in this book, we will focus on the fruit of joy that will be produced in you and through you to the degree that you trust the Holy Spirit completely and allow Him to control your life.

You have learned that you cannot experience the joy of the Lord when you are in control of your life. The Holy Spirit knows how to produce supernatural joy in you and through you. He *will* produce the fruit of joy in your life *if* He truly is in control of your life.

The Holy Spirit is always calm, quiet and confident. You also will be calm, quiet and confident if He is in control of your life. You will not give up your joy if you allow the Holy Spirit to control your life because you trust Him completely.

If the Holy Spirit truly is in control of your life, your life will *not* be controlled by the circumstances you face or by the influence of Satan and his demons. Satan cannot steal joy from the Holy Spirit. Satan cannot steal joy from you if the Holy Spirit truly is in control. If you truly allow the Holy Spirit to control your life, Satan and his demons will go away. They will try to influence other people who have not yielded control of their lives to the Holy Spirit.

This chapter is filled with facts from the holy Bible pertaining to the magnificent life that you can and will lead *if* you gladly give up control of your life and trust completely in the Holy Spirit to do in you and through you what you cannot possibly do yourself. If you are not experiencing the joy of the Lord in your life, go back and meditate on the Scripture in this chapter. *Are you* trusting the Holy Spirit to do in you and through you what you cannot do yourself?

Chapter 30

The Joy of the Lord Is Your Strength

In this chapter we will look into God's Word to see what it says about the relationship between God's joy and God's strength. "...be not grieved and depressed, for the joy of the Lord is your strength and stronghold." (Nehemiah 8:10 AMP)

Please highlight or underline the words "be not grieved and depressed" in this verse of Scripture. God's joy prevents discouragement and depression. Just as darkness cannot be where light is, depression cannot be where joy is.

The Lord will strengthen you when His joy is consistently being manifested in your life. Your heart will sing with joy if you are *absolutely certain* that the supernatural strength of the Lord is available to you.

Absolutely refuse to allow negative emotions to control your life, regardless of the seeming severity of any problems you might face. *Know* that you will receive the supernatural strength of the Lord if you consistently rejoice in the face of adversity. The more joy you have, the stronger you will be. The less joy you have, the weaker you will be.

Jesus Christ is the King of kings and the Lord of lords. He is completely victorious. Know that He lives in your heart. He is with you throughout every minute of every hour of every day of your life (see Matthew 28:20).

If you consistently focus on the indwelling presence of Jesus, you will not lose your joy. You will receive His supernatural strength. "I have strength for all things in Christ Who empowers me [I am ready for anything and equal to anything through Him Who infuses inner strength into me; I am self-sufficient in Christ's sufficiency]." (Philippians 4:13 AMP)

Please highlight or underline the words "I am ready for *anything* and equal to *anything*" in the amplification of this verse of Scripture. You will never face *any* problem that is too difficult for you because Jesus Christ will "infuse inner strength" into you when you have absolute faith in Him.

Meditate on this powerful verse of Scripture when you face difficult problems. Focus on these facts from the holy Bible pertaining to the strength of Jesus Christ. Rejoice continually because you know that Jesus Christ is strengthening you.

You have learned that Satan's mission is to steal, kill and destroy (see John 10:10). Satan and his demons want to steal your joy. The last thing that Satan and his demons want is for you to continually be strong in the Lord. They will do everything they can to attempt to influence you to focus on the problems you face.

You should be so filled with God Himself that your heart overflows with joy. "…be strong in the Lord [be empowered through your union with Him]; draw your strength from Him [that strength which His boundless might provides]." (Ephesians 6:10 AMP)

Please highlight or underline the words "through your union with Him" in the amplification of this verse of Scripture. The strength of the Lord will be manifested in your life to the degree of closeness and intimacy you have with Him. You will draw the supernatural strength from the Lord that "His boundless might provides" if you stay close to Him throughout every day of your life.

Your heart will be filled with joy if you have a close relationship with the Lord and trust Him completely, regardless of the circumstances you face. You should be like the psalmist who said, "My soul melteth for heaviness: strengthen thou me according unto thy word." (Psalm 119:28 KJV)

Please highlight or underline the words "strengthen thou me according unto thy word" in this verse of Scripture. You will receive manifestation of the strength of the Lord if you consistently meditate on Scripture pertaining to the strength of the Lord and the joy of the Lord.

The psalmist received supernatural strength from God's Word when his soul was heavy. The Word of God is supernaturally alive and filled with the mighty power of God (see Hebrews 4:12). If you faithfully obey your Father's instructions to meditate *day and night* on His Word (see Joshua 1:8 and Psalm 1:2-3), your heart will be filled with joy even though you may face seemingly difficult circumstances.

Some Christians give up their joy because they focus on their human weakness and inadequacy when they face difficult problems. Your Father does not expect you to solve every problem with just your limited human abilities (see Isaiah 2:22 and II Corinthians 1:8-9). Receive His strength through faith in Him. "Blessed (happy, fortunate, to be envied) is the man whose strength is in You..." (Psalm 84:5 AMP)

You will receive blessings and happiness from God if you live in God's strength. Praise God and thank Him whenever you face seemingly severe problems. Praise strengthens you spiritually. As you praise the Lord continually whether you feel like praising Him or not, you will find that the joy of the Lord will increase in your life. You will be strengthened as a result.

The more difficult the problems you face may seem, the more you should praise the Lord. You must not allow circumstances to rob you of the joy of the Lord and the strength of the Lord that is fully available to you according to your knowledge of God's Word and your absolute faith in God.

Praise Jesus and thank Him continually for the tremendous victory that He won for you. Thank Him for the victory that you are certain you will receive if you persevere in faith, absolutely refusing to give up your joy. "Sing aloud to God our Strength!..." (Psalm 81:1 AMP)

The psalms are filled with facts about *singing* praises to God in the face of adversity. God is your strength. If you are absolutely certain that He *will* give you the strength you need, you will open your mouth and sing praises to Him regardless of the circumstances you face. You should be like the psalmist who said, "My flesh and my heart faileth: but God is the strength of my heart, and my portion for ever." (Psalm 73:26 KJV)

What did the psalmist do when his flesh and heart failed? He did *not* give up. He turned to the strength of God in his heart. Your Father wants you to do the same. Rejoice continually because you are absolutely certain that God's strength is available to you at all times. "…My grace is sufficient for thee: for my strength is made perfect in weakness. Most gladly therefore will I rather glory in my infirmities, that the power of Christ may rest upon me." (II Corinthians 12:9 KJV)

Please highlight or underline the words "my strength is made perfect *in weakness*" in this verse of Scripture. *Know* that God's strength is perfected in your human weakness. You should be like the apostle Paul who said, "…I take pleasure in infirmities, in reproaches, in necessities, in persecutions, in distresses for Christ's sake: for when I am weak, then am I strong." (II Corinthians 12:10 KJV)

Please highlight or underline the words "I take pleasure in" in this verse of Scripture. *What* did Paul take pleasure in? He took pleasure in the distress and persecution and problems that he faced. *Why* did Paul take pleasure in the adversity he faced? Please highlight or underline the words "when I am weak, then am I strong."

The apostle Paul rejoiced because he was certain that the strength of Jesus Christ would be perfected in his human weakness. He responded with faith and joy to the problems he faced instead of focusing on his human weakness. This same principle applies to you today. "…let the weak say, I am strong [a warrior]!" (Joel 3:10 AMP)

These words do not make any sense whatsoever from a logical and intellectual worldly perspective. Your Father does not want you to live your life from a worldly perspective (see James 4:4, I Corinthians 3:19-20 and I John 2:15-16). He wants your faith in Him and the words that you speak to clearly indicate that you have absolute faith that His supernatural strength always is available to you.

You will not give up your joy if your heart is filled with the supernatural living Word of God as a result of faithfully meditating day and night on the holy Scriptures as your Father has instructed you to do. You will *say* that you are strong even though you are weak in the natural realm. Your thoughts, words and actions will be governed by the Word of God that fills your mind and your heart and pours out of your mouth, regardless of the circumstances you face (see Matthew 12:34).

Joy and strength go together like a hand in a glove. Refuse to allow anything in the world to pull you away from the strength of God. If you focus continually on the strength of God, you will not give up your joy.

This chapter is filled with facts from the holy Bible that explain the relationship between the strength of the Lord and the joy of the Lord. If you are tempted to give up your joy, go back and meditate on these facts from God's Word.

Your Father *will* strengthen you continually if His joy constantly is being released in your life because you praise Him and thank Him regardless of the circumstances you face. Breathe in the joy of the Lord as you live in His presence.

Conclusion

All Christians will experience continual joy throughout eternity in heaven. You will experience supernatural joy from the moment you enter into heaven. However, every Christian does not experience the joy of the Lord here on earth. You must know *exactly* what the Bible instructs you to do to walk in the joy of the Lord. You then must obey these specific instructions to experience the joy of the Lord here on earth.

Some people have a joyful nature from birth. They have been positive and optimistic since they were little children. Other people were much more negative and serious as children. Some children were brought up in a happy home and enjoyed a happy childhood. Other children were brought up in a home that was filled with strife and discord.

Whether you have been happy from birth or not, *you can learn* what the Word of God says about living continually in the joy of the Lord. This book is filled with specific instructions from your Father that tell you exactly what He wants you to do to experience His joy throughout your life on earth.

You should study these verses of Scripture carefully. Romans 12:2 says that your life will be "transformed" if you consistently renew your mind in the Word of God. You must turn away from traditional thinking and the ways of the world. Open your mind. Be willing to accept new concepts from the holy Scriptures pertaining to the joy of the Lord.

People can lose their joy at any age, but we have learned that older people are more liable to lose joy than younger people. Many older people experience more fatigue than they did when they were younger.

As people grow older and experience challenges with their health, they *must* renew their minds continually in God's Word. "…we do not become discouraged (utterly spiritless, exhausted, and wearied out through fear). Though our outer man is [progressively] decaying and wasting away, yet our inner self is being [progressively] renewed day after day." (II Corinthians 4:16 AMP)

Please highlight or underline the words "our outer man is [progressively] decaying and wasting away" in this verse of Scripture and the amplification. Refuse to allow fear, discouragement and exhaustion to rule your life. If your body is "decaying," live in the supernatural joy of the Lord because your "inner self is being [progressively] renewed day after day."

Carefully study the Scripture references in this book pertaining to the joy of the Lord. Fill your mind with this great truth from God. Once this Scripture is in your mind, you then need to meditate on selected verses of Scripture so that your *heart* will be filled with God's Word pertaining to the joy of the Lord.

The joy that your Father placed inside of you when you received Jesus Christ as your Savior must be nurtured continually. This joy will wane and abate if you do not nurture your joy by consistently studying and meditating on God's supernatural living Word.

Your Father has given you many specific instructions telling you exactly what you should do to walk in His joy. Will you do your part? Will you make the quality decision to study God's Word each day and to meditate day and night on these Scripture references pertaining to the joy of the Lord?

If you sincerely desire to walk in the joy of the Lord, you should program your mind and your heart with Scripture much as a computer is programmed. Program yourself each day with *facts* from the holy Bible pertaining to the joy of the Lord.

If you meditate consistently on this Scripture, God's Word in your heart will take authority over anything that is happening in your life. Your heart will sing with joy, regardless of the circumstances you face, because you have faithfully programmed your mind and your heart with instructions and promises from your Father pertaining to His joy.

The Word of God is a seed (see Luke 8:11). If you sincerely desire to experience the harvest of God's joy in your life, you should consistently plant seeds pertaining to the joy of the Lord in your mind and your heart. Jesus said, "...those sown on the good (well-adapted) soil are the ones who hear the Word and receive and accept and welcome it and bear fruit—some thirty times as much as was sown, some sixty times as much, and some [even] a hundred times as much." (Mark 4:20 AMP)

Jesus promised that you will receive a tremendous harvest *if* you consistently plant seeds from God's Word into your mind and your heart. If you faithfully plant these seeds, you will receive a harvest that is thirty, sixty or even a hundred times greater than the seeds of joy you have sown into your mind and your heart by consistently studying and meditating on the holy Scriptures.

Other people will notice the tremendous change in you as you learn and apply these scriptural principles pertaining to the joy of the Lord. This joy is contagious. The more that other people see the joy of the Lord in your life, the more they will want to be around you. They will want to experience the same joy that they see in you.

You can help many people who are going through difficult times to obtain the joy of the Lord. We have provided a quantity discount so that you can purchase several copies of this book (see the order form at the end of this book). Give copies of this book to people who need to learn how to experience the joy of the Lord in their lives.

Help these people to understand that the joy of the Lord is *not* dependent in any way on circumstances they face. Show them how they can experience the wonderful supernatural joy of the Lord that they see in you.

We pray that all of the facts from God's holy Bible in this book have helped you to greatly increase the manifestation of the joy of the Lord in your life. Please share with us a testimony of what this book has meant to you. We have found that we normally need at least three or four paragraphs to consolidate these thoughts into one paragraph to put in our newsletters and on our website to help other people understand that they too can experience the joy of the Lord in their lives.

We would be so pleased to hear from you.

Jack and Judy

Appendix

This book is filled with instructions and promises from God. However, if you have not received Jesus Christ as your Savior, you *cannot understand* the scriptural facts that are contained in this book. "...the mind of the flesh [with its carnal thoughts and purposes] is hostile to God, for it does not submit itself to God's Law; indeed it cannot." (Romans 8:7 AMP)

Please highlight or underline the word "cannot" in this verse of Scripture. If Jesus Christ is not your Savior, you *cannot* understand and obey God's instructions.

People who have not received Jesus Christ as their Savior are not open to the specific instructions God has given us in the Bible. "...the natural, nonspiritual man does not accept or welcome or admit into his heart the gifts and teachings and revelations of the Spirit of God, for they are folly (meaningless nonsense) to him; and he is incapable of knowing them [of progressively recognizing, understanding, and becoming better acquainted with them] because they are spiritually discerned and estimated and appreciated." (I Corinthians 2:14 AMP)

Please highlight or underline the words "does not accept or welcome or admit into his heart the gifts and teachings and revelations of the Spirit of God" in this verse of Scripture. Some people are strongly opposed to the Bible and what it teaches. They look at facts from the Bible as "meaningless nonsense." These people are incapable of learning great spiritual truths from God until and unless they receive Jesus Christ as their Savior.

At the close of this Appendix we will explain exactly what you should do to receive Jesus Christ as your Savior. If and when you make this decision, the glorious supernatural truths of the Bible will open up to you. Jesus said, "…To you it has been given to know the secrets and mysteries of the kingdom of heaven, but to them it has not been given." (Matthew 13:11 AMP)

Please highlight or underline the word "you" in this verse of Scripture. Jesus was speaking to *you* when He said that *you* can "know the secrets and mysteries of the kingdom of heaven."

A spiritual veil blocks all unbelievers from understanding the things of God. "…even if our Gospel (the glad tidings) also be hidden (obscured and covered up with a veil that hinders the knowledge of God), it is hidden [only] to those who are perishing and obscured [only] to those who are spiritually dying and veiled [only] to those who are lost." (II Corinthians 4:3 AMP)

Please highlight or underline the words "hidden (obscured and covered up with a veil that hinders the knowledge of God)" in this verse of Scripture and the amplification. When and if you receive Jesus Christ as your Savior, this spiritual veil will be pulled aside. "…whenever a person turns [in repentance] to the Lord, the veil is stripped off and taken away." (II Corinthians 3:16 AMP)

If you obey the scriptural instructions at the end of this Appendix, Jesus Christ will become your Savior. Everything in your life will become fresh and new. "…if any person is [ingrafted] in Christ (the Messiah) he is a new creation (a new creature altogether); the old [previous moral and spiritual condition] has passed away. Behold, the fresh and new has come!" (II Corinthians 5:17 AMP)

Instead of being opposed to the teachings of the holy Bible, you will be completely open to these teachings. You will have a hunger and thirst to continually learn more truth from the supernatural living Word of God. "…I endorse and delight in the Law of God in my inmost self [with my new nature]." (Romans 7:22 AMP)

Every person who has not received Jesus Christ as his or her Savior is a sinner who is doomed to living throughout eternity in the horror of hell. God has made it possible for *you* to escape this enormous eternal penalty. "…God so loved the world, that he gave his only begotten Son, that whosoever believeth in him should not perish, but have everlasting life." (John 3:16 KJV)

God knew that everyone who lived on earth after Adam and Eve would be a sinner because of the sins of Adam and Eve (see Romans 3:10-12). He sent His only Son Jesus Christ to take upon Himself the sins of the world as He died a horrible death by crucifixion. If you believe that Jesus Christ paid the *full* price for *your* sins and if you trust Him *completely* for your eternal salvation, you will live eternally in the glory of heaven.

There is only *one* way for you to live eternally in heaven after you die – that is to receive eternal salvation through Jesus Christ. "Jesus saith unto him, I am the way, the truth, and the life: no man cometh unto the Father, but by me." (John 14:6 KJV)

If you trust in anyone or anything except Jesus Christ for your eternal salvation, you will not live eternally in heaven. If you are reading these facts about living eternally in heaven because of the price that Jesus Christ has paid for you, you must understand that the same God Who created you actually is *drawing you* to come to Jesus Christ for eternal salvation. Jesus said, "No one is able to come to Me unless the Father Who sent Me attracts and draws him and gives him the desire to come to Me..." (John 6:44 AMP)

Please highlight or underline the words "unless the Father Who sent Me attracts and draws him and gives him the desire to come to Me" in this verse of Scripture. Are you interested in these facts about where you will live throughout eternity? If you are, you can be certain that the same awesome God Who created you is drawing you to Jesus Christ at this very minute.

Heaven is a glorious place. Everyone in heaven is completely healthy and totally happy. "...God shall wipe away all tears from their eyes; and there shall be no more death, neither sorrow, nor crying, neither shall there be any more pain: for the former things are passed away. (Revelation 21:4 KJV)

All of the problems of earth will disappear when you go to heaven. No one in heaven dies. No one in heaven is sad. No one in heaven cries. No one in heaven suffers from any pain.

When you die, you will live eternally in one place or another. If you do not receive Jesus Christ as your Savior, you will live eternally in hell. People in hell will experience continual torment throughout eternity. "...the smoke of their torment ascendeth up for ever and ever: and they have no rest day nor night..." (Revelation 14:11 KJV)

Everyone in heaven is filled with joy. Everyone in hell is miserable. When Jesus described what hell would be like, He said, "...there will be weeping and wailing and grinding of teeth. (Matthew 13:42 AMP)

Throughout eternity the inhabitants of hell will weep and wail. They will grind their teeth in anguish. Can you imagine living this way for the endless trillions of years of eternity? This is *exactly* what will happen to *you* if Jesus Christ is not your Savior.

How do you receive eternal salvation through Jesus Christ? "...if you acknowledge and confess with your lips that Jesus is Lord and in your heart believe (adhere to, trust in, and rely on the truth) that God raised Him from the dead, you will be saved. For with the heart a person believes (adheres to, trusts in, and relies on Christ) and so is justified (declared righteous, acceptable to God), and with the mouth he confesses (declares openly and speaks out freely his faith) and confirms [his] salvation." (Romans 10:9-10 AMP)

You must *believe in your heart* (not just think in your mind) that Jesus Christ paid the full price for all of your sins when He was crucified. You must believe that God raised Jesus from the dead. You must open your mouth and *speak this truth* that you believe in your heart. If you believe in your heart that Jesus Christ died and rose again from the dead and that the price for your sins has been paid for and you tell others that you believe this great spiritual truth, you *have* been saved and you *will* live eternally in heaven.

If Jesus Christ was not your Savior when you began to read this book, we pray that He is your Savior now. Your life will change immensely. You will never be the same again. Every aspect of your life will be gloriously new.

Please contact us and let us know if you have become a child of God by receiving eternal salvation through Jesus Christ. We would like to pray for you and welcome you as our new brother or sister in Christ Jesus. We love you and bless you in the name of our Lord Jesus Christ.

We would be so pleased to hear from you. If you are already a believer, we would be pleased to hear from you as well. We invite you to visit our website at www.lamplight.net. Please let us know if this book or one or more of our other publications has made a difference in your life. Please give us your comments so that we can share these comments in our newsletters and on our website to encourage other people.

Study Guide

What Did You Learn From This Book?

The questions in this Study Guide are carefully arranged to show you how much you have learned about walking in the joy of the Lord at all times, regardless of the circumstances you face. This Study Guide is not an academic test. The sole purpose of the following questions is to help you increase your *practical knowledge* pertaining to the joy of the Lord throughout every day of your life.

Page Reference

A Few Words About Lamplight Ministries

Lamplight Ministries, Inc. originally began in 1983 as Lamplight Publications. After ten years as a publishing firm with a goal of selling Christian books, Lamplight Ministries was founded in 1993. Jack and Judy Hartman founded Lamplight Ministries with a mission of continuing to sell their publications and also to *give* large numbers of these publications free of charge to needy people all over the world.

Lamplight Ministries was created to allow people who have been blessed by our publications to share in financing the translation, printing and distribution of our books into other languages and also to distribute our publications free of charge to jails and prisons. Over the years many partners of Lamplight Ministries have shared Jack and Judy's vision. As the years have gone by, Lamplight Ministries' giving has increased with each passing year. Thousands of people in jails and prisons and in Third World countries have received our publications free of charge.

Our books and Scripture Meditation Cards have been translated into eleven foreign languages – Armenian, Danish, Greek, Hebrew, German, Korean, Norwegian, Portuguese, Russian, Spanish and the Tamil dialect in India. The translations in these languages are not available from Lamplight Ministries in the United States. These translations can only be obtained in the countries where they have been printed.

The pastors of many churches in Third World countries have written to say that they consistently preach sermons in their churches based on the scriptural contents of our publications. We believe that people in several churches in many different countries consistently hear sermons that are based on the scriptural contents of our publications. Praise the Lord!

Jack Hartman was the sole author of twelve Christian books. After co-authoring one book with Judy, Jack and Judy co-authored ten sets of Scripture Meditation Cards. Judy's contributions to *God's Wisdom Is Available To You, Exchange Your Worries for God's Perfect Peace, Unshakable Faith in Almighty God, Receive Healing from the Lord, What Does God Say?, Victory over Adversity* and *God's Joy Regardless of Circumstances* were so significant that she is the co-author of these books. Jack and Judy currently are working on other books that they believe the Lord is leading them to write as co-authors.

We invite you to request our newsletters to stay in touch with us, to learn of our latest publications and to read comments from people all over the world. Please write, fax, call or email us. You are very special to us. We love you and thank God for you. Our heart is to take the gospel to the world and for our books to be available in every known language. Hallelujah!

Lamplight Ministries, Inc.,

PO Box 1307 - Dunedin, Florida, 34697. USA

Phone: 1-800-540-1597 • Fax: 1-727-784-2980

website: lamplight.net • email: lamplight@lamplight.net

We offer you a substantial quantity discount

From the beginning of our ministry we have been led of the Lord to offer the same quantity discount to individuals that we offer to Christian bookstores. Each individual has a sphere of influence with a specific group of people. We believe that you know many people who need to learn the scriptural contents of our publications.

The Word of God encourages us to give freely to others. We encourage you to give selected copies of these publications to people you know who need help in the specific areas that are covered by our publications. See our order form for specific information on the quantity discounts that we make available to you so that you can share our books, Scripture Meditation Cards and CDs with others.

A request to our readers

If this book has helped you, we would like to receive your comments so that we can share them with others. Your comments can *encourage other people* to study our publications to learn from the scriptural contents of these publications.

When we receive a letter containing comments on any of our books, cassette tapes or Scripture Meditation Cards, we prayerfully take out excerpts from these letters. These selected excerpts are included in our newsletters and occasionally in our advertising and promotional materials.

If any of our publications have been a blessing to you, please share your comments with us so that we can share them with others. Tell us in your own words what a specific publication has meant to you and why you would recommend it to others. Please give as much specific information as possible. We prefer three or four paragraphs so that we can condense this into one paragraph.

Thank you for taking a few minutes of your time to encourage other people to learn from the scripture references in our publications.

ORDER FORM FOR BOOKS

Book Title	Quantity	Total
What Does God Say? ($18)	_____ x $18 =	_____
God's Joy Regardless of Circumstances ($14)	_____ x $14 =	_____
Victory Over Adversity ($14)	_____ x $14 =	_____
Receive Healing from the Lord ($14)	_____ x $14 =	_____
Unshakable Faith in Almighty God ($14)	_____ x $14 =	_____
Exchange Your Worries for God's Perfect Peace ($14)	_____ x $14 =	_____
God's Wisdom is Available to You ($14)	_____ x $14 =	_____
Trust God For Your Finances ($10)	_____ x $10 =	_____
What Will Heaven Be Like? ($10)	_____ x $10 =	_____
Quiet Confidence in the Lord ($10)	_____ x $10 =	_____
Never, Never Give Up ($10)	_____ x $10 =	_____
Increased Energy and Vitality ($10)	_____ x $10 =	_____
Conquering Fear ($10)	_____ x $10 =	_____
God's Will for Our Lives ($10)	_____ x $10 =	_____
How to Study the Bible ($7)	_____ x $7 =	_____
Nuggets of Faith ($7)	_____ x $7 =	_____
100 Years From Today ($7)	_____ x $7 =	_____

Price of books _____

Minus 40% discount for 5-9 books _____

Minus 50% discount for 10 or more books _____

Net price of order _____

Add 15% **before discount** for shipping and handling _____

Florida residents only, add 7% sales tax _____

Tax deductible contribution to Lamplight Ministries, Inc. _____

Enclosed check or money order (do not send cash) _____
(Foreign orders must be submitted in U.S. dollars.)

Please make check payable to **Lamplight Ministries, Inc**. and mail to:
PO Box 1307, Dunedin, FL 34697

MC____ Visa____ AmEx____ Disc.____ Card # _____

Exp Date _____ Signature _____

Name _____

Address _____

City _____

State or Province _____ Zip or Postal Code _____

Phone_____ Email _____

ORDER FORM FOR BOOKS

Book Title	Quantity	Total
What Does God Say? ($18)	_____ x $18 =	_____
God's Joy Regardless of Circumstances ($14)	_____ x $14 =	_____
Victory Over Adversity ($14)	_____ x $14 =	_____
Receive Healing from the Lord ($14)	_____ x $14 =	_____
Unshakable Faith in Almighty God ($14)	_____ x $14 =	_____
Exchange Your Worries for God's Perfect Peace ($14)	_____ x $14 =	_____
God's Wisdom is Available to You ($14)	_____ x $14 =	_____
Trust God For Your Finances ($10)	_____ x $10 =	_____
What Will Heaven Be Like? ($10)	_____ x $10 =	_____
Quiet Confidence in the Lord ($10)	_____ x $10 =	_____
Never, Never Give Up ($10)	_____ x $10 =	_____
Increased Energy and Vitality ($10)	_____ x $10 =	_____
Conquering Fear ($10)	_____ x $10 =	_____
God's Will for Our Lives ($10)	_____ x $10 =	_____
How to Study the Bible ($7)	_____ x $7 =	_____
Nuggets of Faith ($7)	_____ x $7 =	_____
100 Years From Today ($7)	_____ x $7 =	_____

Price of books _____

Minus 40% discount for 5-9 books _____

Minus 50% discount for 10 or more books _____

Net price of order _____

Add 15% **before discount** for shipping and handling _____

Florida residents only, add 7% sales tax _____

Tax deductible contribution to Lamplight Ministries, Inc. _____

Enclosed check or money order (do not send cash) _____
(Foreign orders must be submitted in U.S. dollars.)

Please make check payable to **Lamplight Ministries, Inc.** and mail to:
PO Box 1307, Dunedin, FL 34697

MC____ Visa____ AmEx____ Disc.____ Card # _____

Exp Date _____ Signature _____

Name _____

Address _____

City _____

State or Province _____ Zip or Postal Code _____

Phone_____ Email _____

ORDER FORM FOR BOOKS

Book Title	Quantity	Total
What Does God Say? ($18)	_____ x $18 =	_____
God's Joy Regardless of Circumstances ($14)	_____ x $14 =	_____
Victory Over Adversity ($14)	_____ x $14 =	_____
Receive Healing from the Lord ($14)	_____ x $14 =	_____
Unshakable Faith in Almighty God ($14)	_____ x $14 =	_____
Exchange Your Worries for God's Perfect Peace ($14)	_____ x $14 =	_____
God's Wisdom is Available to You ($14)	_____ x $14 =	_____
Trust God For Your Finances ($10)	_____ x $10 =	_____
What Will Heaven Be Like? ($10)	_____ x $10 =	_____
Quiet Confidence in the Lord ($10)	_____ x $10 =	_____
Never, Never Give Up ($10)	_____ x $10 =	_____
Increased Energy and Vitality ($10)	_____ x $10 =	_____
Conquering Fear ($10)	_____ x $10 =	_____
God's Will for Our Lives ($10)	_____ x $10 =	_____
How to Study the Bible ($7)	_____ x $7 =	_____
Nuggets of Faith ($7)	_____ x $7 =	_____
100 Years From Today ($7)	_____ x $7 =	_____

Price of books _____

Minus 40% discount for 5-9 books _____

Minus 50% discount for 10 or more books _____

Net price of order _____

Add 15% **before discount** for shipping and handling _____

Florida residents only, add 7% sales tax _____

Tax deductible contribution to Lamplight Ministries, Inc. _____

Enclosed check or money order (do not send cash) _____
(Foreign orders must be submitted in U.S. dollars.)

Please make check payable to **Lamplight Ministries, Inc**. and mail to:
PO Box 1307, Dunedin, FL 34697

MC____ Visa____ AmEx____ Disc.____ Card # _____

Exp Date _____ Signature _____

Name _____

Address _____

City _____

State or Province _____ Zip or Postal Code _____

Phone_____ Email _____

ORDER FORM FOR BOOKS

Book Title	Quantity	Total
What Does God Say? ($18)	_____ x $18 =	_____
God's Joy Regardless of Circumstances ($14)	_____ x $14 =	_____
Victory Over Adversity ($14)	_____ x $14 =	_____
Receive Healing from the Lord ($14)	_____ x $14 =	_____
Unshakable Faith in Almighty God ($14)	_____ x $14 =	_____
Exchange Your Worries for God's Perfect Peace ($14)	_____ x $14 =	_____
God's Wisdom is Available to You ($14)	_____ x $14 =	_____
Trust God For Your Finances ($10)	_____ x $10 =	_____
What Will Heaven Be Like? ($10)	_____ x $10 =	_____
Quiet Confidence in the Lord ($10)	_____ x $10 =	_____
Never, Never Give Up ($10)	_____ x $10 =	_____
Increased Energy and Vitality ($10)	_____ x $10 =	_____
Conquering Fear ($10)	_____ x $10 =	_____
God's Will for Our Lives ($10)	_____ x $10 =	_____
How to Study the Bible ($7)	_____ x $7 =	_____
Nuggets of Faith ($7)	_____ x $7 =	_____
100 Years From Today ($7)	_____ x $7 =	_____

Price of books _____

Minus 40% discount for 5-9 books _____

Minus 50% discount for 10 or more books _____

Net price of order _____

Add 15% **before discount** for shipping and handling _____

Florida residents only, add 7% sales tax _____

Tax deductible contribution to Lamplight Ministries, Inc. _____

Enclosed check or money order (do not send cash)
(Foreign orders must be submitted in U.S. dollars.) _____

Please make check payable to **Lamplight Ministries, Inc**. and mail to:
PO Box 1307, Dunedin, FL 34697

MC____ Visa____ AmEx____ Disc.____ Card # _____

Exp Date _____ Signature _____

Name _____

Address _____

City _____

State or Province _____ Zip or Postal Code _____

Phone_____ Email _____